D0899047

The Instrumental Music of
Carl Philipp Emanuel Bach

Studies in Musicology, No. 77

George Buelow, Series Editor

Professor of Music
Indiana University

Other Titles in This Series

The Instrumental Music of Carl Philipp Emanuel Bach

by
David Schulenberg

UMI RESEARCH PRESS
Ann Arbor, Michigan

Produced and distributed by
UMI Research Press
an imprint of
University Microfilms International
A Xerox Information Resources Company
Ann Arbor, Michigan 48106

Library of Congress Cataloging in Publication Data

Schulenberg, David.
  The instrumental music of Carl Philipp Emanuel
Bach.

  (Studies in musicology ; no. 77)
  Revision of the author's thesis—State University of
New York at Stony Brook, 1982.
  Bibliography: p.
  Includes index.
  1. Bach, Carl Philipp Emanuel, 1714-1788. Instrumental
music. I. Title. II. Series.

ML410.B16S35 1984   780'.92'4   84-244
ISBN 0-8357-1564-7

Contents

List of Abbreviations

Acta	*Acta musicologica.*
Amal.-Bibl.	Amalien-Bibliothek (the music library of Princess Anna Amalia of Prussia, afterwards incorporated into the former Royal Library in Berlin; see entry below for "P").
B Bc	Brussels. Conservatoire Royal de Musique. Bibliothèque.
B Br	Brussels. Bibliothèque Royale Albert I.
BJ	*Bach-Jahrbuch.*
HV	E.Eugene Helm. *Thematic Catalog of the Works of Carl Philipp Emanuel Bach* (in press). An abbreviated version of the catalog, including a collation with WV (see below), appears as the work-list in *New Grove,* I, pp. 855-62.
JAMS	*Journal of the American Musicological Society.*
JMT	*Journal of Music Theory.*
Kenner and Liebhaber	one of six collections of keyboard works by Bach, published under various titles at Leipzig, 1779-87.
MGG	*Musik in Geschichte und Gegenwart,* ed. Friedrich Blume, 15 vols., suppl. (Kassel, 1949-79).
NV	*Verzeichniss des musikalischen Nachlasses des verstorbenen Capellmeisters Carl Philipp Emanuel Bach* (Hamburg, 1790).
New Grove	*The New Grove Dictionary of Music and Musicians,* ed. Stanley Sadie, 20 vols. (London, 1980).
Notes	*Music Library Association Notes.*
P	manuscript score from the Bach collections of the former Royal Library in Berlin, now divided between the Stiftung Preussischer Kulturbesitz in West Berlin and the Deutsche Staatsbibliothek in East Berlin.
St	manuscript parts from the Bach collections of the former Royal Library in Berlin; see previous entry.
TP	*Le trésor des pianistes,* ed. Aristide and Louise Farrenc, 20 vols. (Paris, 1861-72).

US Wc   Washington, D.C. Library of Congress. Music Collection.
WV   Alfred Wotquenne, *Thematische Verzeichnis der Werke von Carl Philipp Emanuel Bach, (1714-1788)* (Leipzig, 1905).
Wq.n.v.   previously uncatalogued works by Bach listed in Paul Kast, *Die Bach-Handschriften der Berliner Staatsbibliothek* (Trossingen, 1958), pp. 112-3.

Preface

I hope the reader will permit me a few words on the origins of this study. It was as an undergraduate at Harvard that I first made my acquaintance with Emanuel Bach's extraordinary works *für Kenner und Liebhaber,* through Composer-in-Residence and Librarian at Dunster House Charles Kletzsch—or rather through his eighteenth century clavichord, which he generously made available to me. I eventually wrote my bachelor's thesis, under Professor Luise Vosgerchian, on those pieces—an undertaking that had the principal result of convincing me that a fully satisfying discussion of the stylistic problems raised by those pieces would require a comprehensive study of the composer's output. I put the matter aside until similar questions arose some years later in the seminar on eighteenth-century music which I had the privilege of attending under Charles Rosen at the State University of New York at Stony Brook.

My revived ambition to justify the ways of C.P.E. Bach to his critics led to my dissertation on his instrumental music, in which I had invaluable assistance—and criticism—from my adviser, Richard Kramer, and from my readers, harpsichordist Louis Bagger, (J.S.) Bach-scholar Eric Chafe, and Charles Rosen. But I owe my greatest debt—one which I share with all students of Emanuel Bach—to E. Eugene Helm, who, besides offering freely his advice and encouragement, made available to me his nearly complete collection of the works in their principal sources, without which a study such as mine would not have been possible.

This book represents a somewhat streamlined version of the dissertation; I have added new material in Chapter 3 and revised some of my analyses in Chapters 4-7. The dissertation, which I completed in 1982, was written with support furnished by the Graduate School of the State University of New York at Stony Brook. I wish also to thank Judith Kaufman, Music Librarian at Stony Brook, for obtaining many of the items used in writing the original dissertation.

1

Introduction

When the name "Bach" occurred without further specification in the later eighteenth century, it usually meant, depending on the user's geographic and musical orientation, either Carl Philipp Emanuel, Sebastian's second surviving son, or Johann Christian, the youngest of the four composer sons. The very different music of Emanuel and of Christian was known and admired to varying degrees throughout Europe and throughout the period during which tha Viennese Classical style emerged in the mature works of Haydn and Mozart. The music of both was praised even by a critic as set in his tastes as Charles Burney, although his English compatriots favored the anglicized Christian while the Germans patriotically praised the son who had remained in Berlin and later in Hamburg. In this century, overshadowed by the Viennese composers, the Bach sons have been valued chiefly as historical figures, though with ever greater understanding of the chronology and dissemination of various pre-Classical works, and with increasingly sophisticated views of what constitutes stylistic "evolution" and "influence," musicologists have perhaps become less concerned with the historical relationship of Emanuel Bach to Haydn, or of Christian Bach to Mozart, than with the music of the two composers considered for its own sake. Christian's important output includes symphonies and chamber music, on the one hand, and operas and other vocal works on the other, although the significance of the latter is as yet suggested only in the bare list of works in his catalog. No one disputes the consummate grace and beauty of Christian's music, though by comparison with the superficially similar music of Mozart it is, as Charles Rosen notes, "a little empty."[1] Emanuel, unlike his younger brother, seems to have written practically nothing but instrumental music until well into his musical maturity. Despite a few large religious works and many *Lieder* of some importance, his fame rightly lies in his instrumental compositions, especially those involving keyboard instruments. Compared to that of Christian, Emanuel's style is less easily gratifying, demanding patience, understanding, and wit of both performer and listener, not to mention a deeper emotional involvement than that of any other member of Bach's generation except perhaps Gluck, his exact contemporary, or his older brother Wilhelm Friedemann. While much of Emanuel's best music has been available in print for at least several decades, and a few works are now even performed with some regularity, his style remains difficult for many listeners, and even his best works, as a result, tend to be admired (or disliked) for superficial or inconsequential reasons.

Musical style is a difficult phenomenon to explain or define. Rosen suggests that "the concept of a style creates a mode of understanding,"[2] that is, a means whereby individual works can be quickly placed within a context and thus more confidently comprehended. The style itself might be understood more or less broadly, e.g., the style of Western tonal music, the Classical style, the style of Haydn's Opus 33 Quartets. But in any case the sense of the style arises from a familiarity with a number of related works, and this makes possible a quicker and fuller understanding of unfamiliar works which are perceived as belonging to the same style. Any effort to describe or analyze a particular style must, of course, proceed primarily from the works themselves, although other sources of information—especially contemporary theory and criticism—may also prove useful. But description of a style must be both more and less than a series of analyses of individual pieces: less, because it cannot be overly concerned with the peculiarities of single works, more because it purports to give precepts which will aid in the understanding of a large body of music.

That assignment to a style might be an *impediment* to the understanding of a certain repertory is not immediately obvious. But this becomes possible when the work or repertory under scrutiny is viewed in inappropriate terms or—what amounts to the same thing—is misidentified with respect to its style. One would gain a distorted view, at best, by hearing or analyzing a concerto by Sebastian Bach in terms of a Mozart concerto. More difficult is the case with transitional or eclectic repertories, where a composer seems to make use of elements drawn from several different styles, each of which may be individually familiar. Such works will not necessarily conform to the patterns or meet the expectations of any of the styles to which they seem to refer. In the twentieth century the neo-classic works of Stravinsky raise such problems, perhaps intentionally. With certain composers of the eighteenth century, however, the impression of stylistic "inconsistencies" or "unresolved conflicts"—to use expressions which have been applied to one pre-Classical composer[3]—may be an undesirable by-product of the modern analyst's point of view, or worse, of a real lack of sympathy with the work's actual style. Needless to say, it is essential in any critical or analytical exercise to understand works on their own terms and not those of preceding or succeeding periods.

Considerations of this sort arise almost inevitably with the music of Emanuel Bach. But are the difficulties in the music intrinsic to it or do they arise only when it is heard in an inappropriate way? If genuine, are they necessarilly blemishes, or even signs of the composer's incompetence, or do they play an essential role in the fulfillment of legitimate formal or expressive aspirations? In short, are Bach's most characteristic works truly incoherent, as has been claimed, and if so could they have been made any more coherent without losing their special charm and expressive power?

Ultimately , answers to such questions rest on how one defines a term such as "incoherent." Many writers seem to have assumed that the apparent eclecticism of Bach, like that of other composers whose careers peaked around 1750, necessarily leaves his music inadequately integrated at some deep structural level. Philip Barford, a sensitive proponent of Bach as a prototypical Romantic composer, emphasizes the apparent conflicts in the style:

> a somewhat self-conscious intellectualism, leading to formal experimentation . . . the use of thematic contrast which sometimes rises to the level of dramatic antithesis, but more often to a fragmentary style not unified by an overall rhythmic flow; a vein of 'sentimental rhetoric' (Tovey), often tedious, but sometimes achieving great depths of romantic feeling.[4]

Somewhat in the same vein, Jan LaRue finds that:

> C. Ph. E. Bach's place in the development of the classical style is an enigmatic paradox; while he belongs among the most respected and most influential personalities of the eighteenth century, as much as a composer as a theorist, he does not always succeed in coordinating all musical elements (*Faktoren*) in the full classical sense . . . he combines baroque, classical, and romantic characteristics in a singularly fascinating combination which rarely, however, leads to a truly gratifying synthesis.[5]

Without denying the validity of the observations that led to these and like-minded assessments, I would prefer to discuss Bach's style without referring to separate "Baroque" or "Classical" components. That is not to say that the music cannot be unfavorably criticized, or cannot be compared with works in earlier or later styles. But it does imply the necessity of avoiding the type of analysis that merely identifies isolated elements of the style and equates them with elements of other more familiar styles. Such an approach inevitably tends toward creating an impression of eclecticism or even incoherence in the music.

As Rosen has suggested, Emanuel's music is entirely successful when considered on its own terms: "It is a pity not to accept the standards it lays down for itself."[6] This study represents an experiment to define those terms, Bach's own "standards" if one wishes to call them that. To that end I have largely avoided comparison between his music and that of his contemporaries. I have not, however, taken the other extreme and adopted the quixotic goal of analyzing the music solely in terms of "itself." In analyzing any work one adopts a point of view, a context, which gives meaning to what is analyzed, and which begins by establishing *what* in particular is to be described. My context here has been formed (in part) from certain eighteenth century musical theory and criticism, some of it referring specifically to the music of C.P.E. Bach or related composers; these writings are the subject of Chapter 3. I have made a special point *not* to seek in Bach's music anything that might support his oft-alleged significance in the "evolution" of Classical sonata form, nor have I used a study of his music as a vehicle for investigating specific theoretical problems or as a demonstration of the powers of a given analytical method. Most previous studies of Bach's music have been burdened in one such way or another, or else have been intentionally limited to a small fraction of his output—selected keyboard sonatas, for example, or the chamber music. Here I have tried to be as comprehensive as possible while making an effort to point out, through my choices of musical examples, particularly outstanding or unusual works.

Before proceeding to the music itself it is necessary to discuss a few preliminary matters, especially the manner in which Bach's works are cited in the following pages. Until now Bach has been blessed, and musicologists cursed, by a proliferation of catalogs and numbering systems that will finally be superseded by the one in preparation by E. Eugene Helm *(HV)*.[7] The most important of the older lists are the catalog of the composer's estate *(NV)*,[8] which includes a list of works probably drawn from the composer's own catalog, and the thematic catalog drawn up by Alfred Wotquenne in 1905 *(WV)*, which is essentially a list of the important (but by no means complete) holdings of the Royal Conservatory in Brussels. Supplementing this list is that of Paul Kast for works in the Berlin libraries attributed to Bach and not in *WV*; items in Kast's catalog bear the prefix *Wq.n.v.* [9]

Wotquenne's catalog numbers are the best known, but they will eventually have to give way to those of Helm's far more complete and accurate catalog. Wotquenne's numbering remains useful in one respect, however—it assigns a single number to each of Bach's publications, simplifying reference to certain groups of pieces that each receive their own number in Helm's catalog. But except when referring to such collections, the most convenient procedure will be to cite the numbers of both *HV* and *WV* for each work referred to. The first number in each citation will be that of the principal entry under which the work falls, followed, where necessary, by the number of the individual work within the entry, the number of the movement, and then the appropriate measure numbers. Thus a passage in the finale of the sixth Württemberg Sonata would be designated as H. 36 *(W. 49/6)* 3/1-8.

Despite the possibilities for confusion in the various catalogs, Bach's instrumental works are not particularly numerous for an eighteenth-century composer, and they have been relatively well preserved. On the other hand, most of the Hamburg church music has probably been lost irretrievably with the near-complete disappearance during World War II of the library of the Berlin Singakademie. Apparently the only significant lacuna in the instrumental *oeuvre* is the product of the dispersal of the early versions of those concertos, sonatas, and trio-sonatas which Bach is known to have revised at Berlin during the 1740's, a total of some twenty-eight works. Bach's own copies of these early versions may well have been among the "ream or more of [his] old compositions" which Bach himself destroyed in 1786.[10] A few, at least, survive in peripheral sources and have been identified with reasonable certainty, though in some cases only through skillful detective work.[11]

2

Emanuel Bach and the Eighteenth Century

Bach's apparently uneventful life falls conveniently into three periods: his student years at Leipzig and Frankfurt-an-Oder, which saw the compositions dated 1731 to 1738;[1] his thirty years in the service of Frederick the Great (chiefly in Berlin) until early in 1768[2]; and his twenty remaining years as cantor at the Johanneum and director of music in the five chief churches of Hamburg, a position in which he succeeded his godfather, Georg Philipp Telemann. In the ultimate church appointment, Emanuel's career mirrors that of his father. But Emanuel's success in finding a gratifying position marked the fulfillment of a wish denied his father, and in other respects the biographies of the two have little in common. Even at Hamburg, Emanuel apparently produced little original church music; much of the music he presented as cantor and in the churches consisted of pastiches from various sources.[3] The preceding years as an instrumentalist in royal service occupied a far greater portion of Emanuel's life than the somewhat similarly-occupied years of his father (at Cöthen and Weimar) did in his. Moreover, Emanuel was not held in high regard by his royal patron, at least not in the later years of Emanuel's employment at Berlin, during which the only music heard at court seems to have been that of Frederick himself and of his flutist, Quantz.[4]

Thus at both Berlin and Hamburg Bach was essentially independent as a composer, at least in the sense that he was not under obligation to compose regularly in any particular style or genre. As a consequence, such changes as occurred in his style over the course of his career cannot be related directly to changes of locale or employment. There is no clear division, equally evident in all important genres, between music of the first few Berlin years and that of the immediately preceding period. Instead, a surge of impressive writing in several genres (concerto, sonata and trio-sonata) begins a few years *after* Bach's establishment at Berlin—around 1742-1748—and again toward the end of the Berlin years, in the early 1760's. It was also during the mid-forties that Bach made his systematic revision of earlier works, usually by adding embellishments, occasionally by interpolating new material.

Darrell Berg, writing on the sonatas, speaks of this earlier Berlin period (through 1749) as an "abnormally" long period of "expansion" marked by growth in Bach's "control of methods of expansion and elaboration."[5] For Berg, this is followed by a period of "refinement" during the remaining Berlin years, which form "a plateau in the evolution of Bach's style."[6] But Bach is already a complete master in such works as the D-minor concerto of 1748, H. 427 (*W. 23*), the Trio-Sonata in E from 1749, H. 581 (*W. 162*), or the Württemberg sonatas (W. 49), written as early as 1742-1744. All these works share expansive proportions and ambitious expressive aspirations, in both respects surpassing the typical work of the 1750's, when Bach often seems to slip into a relatively relaxed, merely fluent, manner.

Indeed, the fifties and early sixties saw not merely refinement but a real change of style, symbolized by the new types of setting to which Bach turned his attention. These years saw a dwindling number of trio-sonatas and only one non-keyboard solo sonata, the harp sonata of 1762, H. 564 (*W. 139*). Bach instead seems to have been occupied by the writing of the *Versuch über die wahre Art das Clavier zu spielen,* issued in two volumes that appeared in 1753 and 1762; during this period he composed numerous little keyboard pieces that must have been used in teaching. Among them are several dozen character pieces with French titles, though few are particularly close to contemporary French models in form or style.[7] Bach's sharp eye for means of improving his financial situation[8] may have been one reason for the increasing number of what the Germans call *Modesonaten*, although these generally slight works also could have been employed by students. To the pedagogic impulse one might trace as well those works furnished with written-out variations of repeated sections; Bach began to compose such pieces in earnest in 1757 with the Sonatas H. 135 (*W. 65/32*) and H. 126 (*W. 50/5*).[9] Varied reprises continued thereafter to be an obsession of Bach's, particularly in the so-called *Reprisen-Sonaten* (W. 50), published in 1760, and in the fifteen Sonatines for keyboard and orchestra (H. 449-64; *W. 96-110*), a unique but disappointing set of pieces which occupied Bach from 1762 to 1764.

Most of the later Berlin works display "refinement," but with few exceptions they lack the compelling musical ideas or intense expressivity of the strongest works of the forties. Toward the end of the Berlin period, especially among the unpublished keyboard sonatas, there is perhaps a turning back toward a more serious style. In the keyboard works of the Hamburg period, particularly those published in the collections "für Kenner und Liebhaber," there is a marked concision in the presentation of musical ideas, as well as some radical harmonic explorations. At the same time there is some relaxation in Bach's usually quite stylized formal procedures, particularly in some of the concertos and symphonies. Such freedom has its best known examples in the rondos and fantasias of the *Kenner und Liebhaber* series; of two of these fantasias, Bach said that they were written down and published "so that after my death one could see what a *Fantast* I was."[10] But Bach's *Fantasie* is equally evident in other works of the period, notably several of the piano trios, the three

"Quartets" for flute, viola and keyboard, H. 538-540 (*W. 93-5*),[11] and the last ten symphonies, which are his most important efforts in this genre.

While following the general outline just sketched, Bach's composing career does not fall into easily delineated style periods, and it is impossible to speak of a uniform development of style occurring simultaneously in all genres. While producing sonatas and concertos more or less continuously throughout his career,[12] Bach favored other types of pieces only at certain periods: flute sonatas during the first ten years at Berlin, character pieces and pedagogic works for keyboard during the fifties, piano trios (all thirteen of them) in the three-year period 1775-1777. These patterns are not necessarily related to Bach's stylistic development; intensive work in a given genre may only reflect the influence of a particular patron or the momentary fashionability of a particular type of piece.[13] Moreover, Bach tends to conform to the stylistic expectations associated with each type—hence the use of imitative counterpoint in most of the trio-sonatas, which tend to be the most conservative of Bach's major works. Because each genre establishes its own patterns, nearly contemporary works in different categories may seem decades apart in style—for example, the quasi-Baroque sonata for harpsichord and viola, H. 511 (*W. 88*), from 1759, and the brilliant G-major Symphony H. 656 (*W. 180*) from the preceding year.[14] Even within a given genre, great gaps separate the inoffensive *galanterie* of the Sonata H. 77 *(W. 62/14)* of 1753, and the experimentalism of the *Probestücke* (H. 70-75; *W. 63/1-6*) of the previous year.

Such contrasts recall a passage in Bach's autobiography to the effect that only a small portion of his work reflected his personal interests.[15] The rest—works composed to order or for teaching, one presumes—include many of the individually published sonatas of W. 62 and most of the little keyboard pieces, not to mention arrangements of the latter for everything from wind bands to musical clocks. But it would be dangerous always to equate Bach's aesthetic values with ours. He surely placed what seems today an excessive value on the variation of repeated passages, producing a number of works whose insignificance is hardly lessened by the pains Bach took to write out varied reprises.[16] Similarly, the bland counterpoint of many long trio-sonata movements may have been less bothersome to Bach than to us; despite gestures toward the polyphonic tradition, they employ the essentially homophonic *galant* style favored at Berlin.

In his autobiography Bach is especially critical of what he calls the comic style (*das Komische*),[17] a formulation which, if originally confined to comic opera, might have applied as well to most of the instrumental music issued in the later eighteenth century.[18] It is quite possible that the "comic," in Bach's mind, included much of the emerging Viennese Classical repertoire. Mozart, whose *Entführung aus dem Serail* was performed at Brunswick by Friedrich Bach,[19] would probably have been regarded by Emanuel chiefly as a composer for the comic theater; he is mentioned, along with Bach's friend Georg Benda, as one of the composers whose works were presented on the Hamburg stage during the 1770's.[20] Haydn's music is said to have then been unpopular in Hamburg, owing to its mixture of the serious and the comic, "particularly as there is more of the latter than the former in his work."[21] Yet the combination of "serious" and "comic" techniques is the very essence of Classical style; the supreme example is the Finale of Mozart's *Jupiter* Symphony, which combines strict fugue and canon with the formulas of comic opera. Bach is known to have listened approvingly to at least two of Haydn's works—from the "Opus 33" quartets[22]—which suggests that Bach was able to distinguish between a superficial "comic" style and the more profound examples of the new Viennese style.

In fact Bach reserves his greatest disdain for the popular genres of accompanied clavier sonata and rondo,[23] and his works include only a few insignificant examples for keyboard with one accompany ing instrument.[24] On the other hand, rondos are frequent among Bach's clavier *pièces* and in movements from lighter sonatas. In the Hamburg period the rondo form leads to some of his most extraordinary products. Schleuning, taking some of Bach's statements perhaps too literally,[25] assumes that Bach's published works, even some of the late rondos and fantasies, could not have employed the "full art of the composer and complete freedom of the imagination (*Fantasie)*" because they were intended for public consumption.[26] This seems too harsh a judgment; the works "für Kenner und Liebhaber" seem a successful blend of simple "comic" musical ideas for the *Liebhaber* and sophisticated and subtle harmony, modulation and phrasing for the *Kenner*.[27] To be sure, Emanuel's seriousness of purpose is not always immediately evident; the late rondos usually begin with several relatively simple periodic statements of the theme and *couplets* before beginning their distant tonal excursions. In such pieces Bach translates the "comic" into something serious, as Haydn and Mozart frequently do also.

Rosen and Landon both discuss the acceptance of popular idioms into concert music of the later eighteenth century.[28] It is, of course, only one aspect of what Newman calls the "style shift" from Baroque to Classical.[29] Rosen summarizes the shift as occurring in two large waves:

> the first, from approximately 1730 to 1765, in which the textures of the previous style were radically simplified; and then, from 1765 to 1795, a second and equally profound change in which the new forms and textures were given a greater monumentality and complexity.[30]

To be sure, the "previous," that is, Baroque, style, was not necessarily complex in texture, particularly in the Italian opera which was one of the chief sources of the *galant* manner.[31] But even the simplest such music generally retains an independent bass line, and perhaps a real tenor part as well. In any case,

Emanuel's participation in the transition described by Rosen is largely limited to the first "wave," notably in his adoption of simple *galant* textures and increasingly periodic phrasing in the fifties—though without abandoning a complexity of harmony and rhythmic gesture inherited from Sebastian Bach.

The newer elements of style adopted by Emanuel Bach tend to lie fairly close to the musical surface. One frequently cited aspect of the "style shift," an increased flexibility in dynamics, is clearly demonstrated in the proliferation of dynamic indications in Bach's first three published sets of sonatas.[32] But the increasing variety of dynamic markings does not correspond with any significant change in texture or in the character of the motion; the dynamics are employed chiefly to indicate accents, echoes, and similar events whose existence in earlier music is already implicit. A more significant shift in style is Bach's occasional adoption of a "symphonic style:" a type of extrovert, harmonically and melodically forthright manner derived from the Italian opera *sinfonia* and imitated frequently in other *genres*, especially the keyboard sonatas, beginning in the mid-forties.[33] Still, the forms of these works, and the means of articulating them, remain quite the same as in other "non-symphonic" works.

Those primarily textural shifts adopted by Bach are manifestations of the type of writing frequently called *galant*, regarded by many writers as an important step toward the Classical style.[34] Recently the term *galant* has received some clarification. Berg understands it in the customary way: "an affable, uncomplicated manner of writing in which moderately expressive elements were acceptable and affective extremes avoided."[35] This definition stems from Johann Adolph Scheibe's description of a "moderate and galant manner of writing" which is witty, pleasant, and flowing, with a natural (*ungezwungen*) melody which nonetheless includes various types of ornaments and embellishments.[36] But David Sheldon has shown that, despite a bewildering variety of vaguely approbative meanings in the early part of the century, by 1750 or so, *galant* had acquired a more specific meaning, at least as used by the theorists of the Berlin school.[37] For Marpurg, Türk and Kirnberger—to whose names one might add Bach and Koch—*Galant* is the free style of opera, solo keyboard and chamber music, as opposed to the strict or *gebunden* style of fugues and church music. Sheldon's finding bears specifically on the character of the voice-leading; he associates the *galant* with Heinichen's "theatrical" treatment of dissonance, which permits certain mild dissonances to enter unprepared.[38] Quantz, moreover, tells us that quartets (pieces with three *obligato* parts plus continuo) require more intricate counter-point than trios, leaving the latter more apt for the expression of *galant* ideas.[39] Sheldon's interpretation is borne out by some details in the music of the Berlin composers. A characteristic cadential formula treats the antepenultimate 6/4-chord as an appoggiatura; that is, the fourth, which in strict counterpoint is a dissonance demanding downward resolution, is permitted to ascend to the fifth in the following dominant chord in examples from the theorists as well as in actual practice. While displaying such *galant* licenses with regularity, the Berlin style also conforms with the less technical sense of the word *galant*, especially in the simplified texture and harmony and in the corresponding emotional moderation, both of which often cross over into vapidity.

Ex. 2-1.   a)   F.W. Marpurg, *Kritische Briefe über die Tonkust,*
vol. 2 (Berlin, 1763), p. 9.

b)   C.P.E. Bach, Sonata in E minor for flute and
continuo (1737), H. 551 (*W. 124*) 3/7-8.

Emanuel's less personal works include instances of the anonymous Berlin style, but his reputation rests now, as it did in the eighteenth century, on those pieces that represent his personal version of the *galant*, now often referred to as the *Empfindsamkeit*. The latter, unlike *galant*, is apparently a twentieth-century term, at least as applied to music. Berg found the similar word *empfindlich* used as a late eighteenth-century equivalent for the English "sentimental"—without the derogatory implications now attached to the latter—but concluded that Bach's music "was probably not described as *empfindsam* during the eighteenth century."[40] Newman regards the *Empfindsamkeit* as

a special case of the *galant* style . . . an intensification and exaggeration . . . The harmonic vocabulary, dynamic fluctuations, and articulatory minutae are all increased. And the tonal outlines are colored by surprising key contrasts.[41]

Yet the term seems to refer more to an aspiration toward certain types of emotional expression than to any specific musical means of attaining them. Newman's description might apply to any number of eighteenth-century works of heightened expressivity, particularly those in minor keys.

Similar aspirations among a number of early Classical composers, including the young Haydn and Mozart, have been interpreted as the products of an "Austrian musical crisis" beginning in the 1760's, roughly two decades after the first important *empfindsam* works of Emanuel Bach.[42] This Austrian *Sturm und Drang* has been traced by Lothar Hoffmann-Erbrecht to the composers of the North German school; he understands *Sturm und Drang* in quasi-political terms, as "a stormy rejuvenation of culture [*Kulturverjungung*] which proclaimed a new sensibility [*Lebensgefühl*] in protest against the Enlightenment and the sentimentality of the Rococo."[43] The beginning of this movement (*Bewegung*), as Hoffmann-Erbrecht terms it, is dated "with confidence" to the years 1750-1765, and therefore coincides with such works as the six *Probestuck* sonatas of 1753. But Bach already had written some of his most intensely expressive works during the forties, and there is little documentary evidence for the ideological reaction against the music of the rococo envisioned by Hoffmann-Erbrecht. If the term *Sturm und Drang* is to be applied to music at all, it is probably better to confine the term to those Austrian works to which it is usually applied. Bach's stormiest and most self-consciously dramatic works retain *galant* textures and Baroque affective mannerisms, while bearing few demonstrable direct relationships with such pieces as Haydn's *Lamentazione* symphony (Hob. I: 23) or Mozart's early G-minor symphony, K. 183 (173dB).

A more useful term for characterizing Bach's style is *mannerism*. In her depiction of Bach as a mannerist, Berg seems to follow Rosen, who has referred to the circle of composers around Bach as the "North German mannerists."[44] Elsewhere Rosen has written:

> It is the lack of any integrated style, equally valid in all fields, between 1755 and 1775 that makes it tempting to call this period 'mannerist'. . . In order to surmount the problem of style that faced them, the composers of that time were reduced to cultivating a highly individual manner.[45]

In Emanuel's case, the stimulus toward adopting a "highly individual manner" probably lay in the mutually contradictory inspirations of his father's music and the current *galant* and "theatrical" types. Robert Marshall has pointed out the hitherto unappreciated degree to which Sebastian Bach adopted current fashions into his personal style in such late works as the B-minor Mass and the Musical Offering.[46] Thus it may be wrong to understand the collision of *galant* simplicity and Baroque counterpoint as *necessarily* leading to mannerism or incoherence. While retaining certain distinctive elements of his father's personal style, such as the expressive chromatic harmony and the scrupulously written-out melodic embellishment, Emanuel neglected others, such as the flexibility of form that permits the structure of a fugue, for example, to follow from the contrapuntal possibilities of its subject. Thus Emanuel's style is the product of his own continuing development of certain late Baroque techniques, but within an essentially unchanging approach to rhythm, form, and the relationship of structure and material.

The style that emerges is sufficiently distinct from the Baroque to merit the label *mannerist*—and not only because of its reliance on a few easily recognized conventions which, in a discussion of the *galant* in general, Newman calls "decided mannerisms."[47] The term *mannerist* has been applied to at least two other styles or repertories, and it is from these that one gains some idea of how the term might be applied to Emanuel Bach. Maria Rika Maniate's study of mannerism in sixteenth-century music emphasizes the use of *maniera*: essentially, a personal style achieved through technical devices or conceits meant to elicit surprise or admiration while being expressive or witty or both.[48] Berg's study of Bach as mannerist leans heavily on this conception, which involves identifying individual events or techniques, chiefly in the musical surface, as manifestations of Bach's *maniera*.

Quite another "expression of the mannerist principle" occurs in the so-called *ars subtilior* of the late fourteenth and early fifteenth century, though it is described by Willi Apel in terms that might apply to any "mannered" style: "deliberate diversification, extravagance, and utmost complexity."[49] Apel's understanding of this style gets to the heart of musical mannerism, for he recognizes in it a basic texture largely preserved from the preceding *ars nova* style: "a two-voice framework that can be reduced to traditional progressions of perfect and imperfect consonances."[50] Moreover, the forms of the *ars subtilior* are usually expanded versions of the established *formes fixes*, lacking any new essential features. Hence the "mannerism" lies in a profuse embellishment of the underlying form and texture, drawing the ear away from the work's true structure.

Relatively simple structure and texture may stand beneath the most manneristic surface. Sudden changes of motion in the surface may disguise or embellish a deeper harmonic rhythm that is unchanging—a point demonstrated in Chapter 5—though this may leave the music open to Vrieslander's charge of a "fatal mixture of styles."[51] Miesner explains this as an inevitable characteristic of music composed in a transitional period (*Übergangszeit*).[52] LaRue points to a similar explanation in his concept of "style stratification," which he uses to analyze the "puzzling phenomenon of a composer to whom we respond strongly as far as his melody is concerned, yet about whom in other respects we feel strangely blocked and frustrated."[53] But it is not enough merely to identify certain aspects of a work as "Baroque" and others as "Classical." One must show explicitly how the "Baroque" aspects prevent the "Classical" ones from having their full effect, or why certain musical elements, each characteristic of one of the two periods, cannot co-exist in an integrated whole, bearing in mind the possibility of mannerism itself as a unified style.

Descriptions of Bach's music as manneristic, or charges of "style stratification" leveled against it, are possible only by reference to the music of other eighteenth-century composers. As a long-lived musician active in Northern Europe's two most important musical centers, Emanuel had ample opportunity to influence, and to be influenced by, most of the major figures of the century. One would expect Sebastian Bach, the only teacher whom Emanuel acknowledged,[54] to have been a decisive influence, yet the divergence of all the sons from the father in matters of style is common knowledge. Sebastian's own special relationship to the *galant* style suggests that significant connections between his music and that of his sons (especially Friedemann and Emanuel) have been overlooked. Emanuel's mastery of chromatic harmony and written-out embellishment indicates a closer relationship than is sometimes assumed; in addition, specific references to Sebastian's music occur occasionally in Emanuel's early works, though without the elder composer's contrapuntal sophistication. E.H. Beurmann noted the obvious thematic identity between Sebastian's two-part Invention in F and Emanuel's earliest surviving sonata, H. 2 (*W. 62/1*).[55] In fact Emanuel frequently emulates his father's polyphony, though the result is usually a compromise between real independence of voices and *galant* homophony.

Yet Sebastian's most important influence must have been as a teacher rather than as a model for imitation. Indeed, some of the weaknesses in Emanuel's music may have stemmed from the emphasis in his father's pedagogy on certain aspects of composition at the expense of others. One such aspect is the technique of melodic composition through the "variation" or composing-out of harmonies (discussed in the following chapter), which may have been responsible for Emanuel's over-reliance on melodic embellishment in many works as a primary focus of interest. Another may be Emanuel's self-limitation in most works to an unvarying type of sonata form regardless of the nature of the material or setting. Though typical of the mid-century composers as a group, this formalism, as Berg calls it,[56] could also have been inherited through Sebastian Bach. In the process of producing church works on a regular schedule during the early Leipzig years, Sebastian worked out a more or less routine method of setting the texts of most arias and choruses. As Marshall has shown, Sebastian's approach to form (and other matters as well) in such pieces is far more schematized than in the instrumental works, which were written at greater leisure.[57] Perhaps it was the routine, a product of necessity and hard experience, rather than the extraordinary, that Sebastian passed on to his sons and students.

Of course, Sebastian as well as his students must have recognized the unfashionability of the older composer's personal manner, and for stylistic models at the more superficial levels of structure, Emanuel would have looked elsewhere. It is surprising that the most obvious of many possible sources is rarely mentioned, that is, Telemann.[58] In fact it would be hard to imagine any German composer of Bach's generation who was not influenced by Telemann, whose instrumental works are frequently cited by the theorists of the time and whose vocal works were occasionally performed by Sebastian Bach at Leipzig.[59] There is little space here to give concrete examples of stylistic resemblance; one might note that Telemann, like Emanuel, tends toward a certain sort of clever humor, in occasional eccentric modulations and rhythmic irregularities. Similarities between the two composers are clearest in the trio-sonatas: long quasi-fugal opening expositions, relaxation afterwards into *galant* parallel thirds or sixths or into soloistic passage-work, and the type of sequence which Marpurg calls canonic.[60] This is not to say that Telemann was the inventor of such techniques, but he was certainly among the most prolific and best known authors using them.

Among other influences, writers have mentioned Tartini on the concertos[61] and François Couperin on the keyboard music,[62] but in neither case is there anything in Bach's music that can be taken as coming directly from one of the two earlier composers. LaRue speaks, with greater justice, of Adolf Hasse as the "Senior" of the North German composers of symphonies, among whom Bach figures prominently,[63] but Hasse's influence on the symphony was chiefly a by-product of his role as the most prestigious composer of *opera seria* in Germany. Hasse, who spent most of his career in Dresden, was the model (by royal decree) for Carl Heinrich Graun in Berlin, and in fact the two Graun brothers, together with the flutist Quantz, are more obvious candidates for direct influence on Bach.[64] Their symphonies and chamber music must have been familiar to Bach, whose own works follow the conventions of form and order of movements established by them. But of these composers only Johann Gottlieb Graun (1702/3-71) seems to have had genuine originality, and his best works, among them several ambitious *empfindsam* trio-sonatas, may have been products of a stylistic development that paralleled rather than influenced Bach's own.

Bach's stylistic relationships with younger composers are similarly problematical. His one truly distinguished student was his youngest brother Christian, who lived and studied with him in Berlin for several years after their father's death. Though Christian learned enough from his older brother to write several keyboard concertos in a thoroughly competent imitation of the Berlin style, he soon abandoned his brother's tutelage, religion, and seriousness of intent.[65] Christian later made a strong impression on the young Mozart when the latter met him in England in 1764, but by then Christian's style had become thoroughly Italianized. Thus, despite the oft-cited gestures of respect made toward Bach by each of the Viennese triumvirate,[66] it is probably wrong to seek any direct link between them and Emanuel Bach. It is of great interest to know that Haydn owned a score of Bach's Double-Concerto, H. 479 (*W. 47*), written out by Bach's chief copyist, Michel,[67] and that Mozart, twice in the winter of 1788, performed Bach's *Auferstehung und Himmelfahrt Jesu*,[68] but such connections between important composers only reflect their respect and perhaps some vague sort of influence by inspiration. Efforts to link Bach with the Romantics, [69] on grounds of common expressive aspirations, are even less convincing, since their musical procedures have little in common even if the aesthetic climates in which the works were written had similarities. No claims are made here for the historical significance of Emanuel's music—indeed, the contrary is suggested. But musical value and historical significance do not necessarily go hand in hand.

3

The Theoretical and Literary Background:
Eighteenth-Century Writing on Music in Germany

While any study of eighteenth-century music may be deepened by some attention to contemporaneous theoretical or literary sources, it is worthwhile to bear in mind the problems inherent in applying any theory or criticism to the works of art that appeared at the same time. Writers may express outdated ideas or uninformed prejudices, and their interests or aesthetics may differ greatly from those of the modern reader. Much of the eighteenth-century musical literature, whether theoretical or critical—to make a not always useful distinction—is directed toward a reader who is liberally educated but not necessarily well-versed in music. The writer may be attempting elementary instruction in composition or performance, or in both, but in any case cannot be expected to write at the sophisticated level necessary to explain the subtleties of, say, a rondo by Emanuel Bach. Even the most advanced works, such as Bach's *Versuch* or some of Marpurg's treatises, only incidentally treat of material that is of use to a modern historian or analyst. Thus the eighteenth-century writings can suggest channels of speculation or re-open perspectives that are now unfamiliar, but they will not provide direct answers for most of the questions that concern the modern reader.

Fortunately for a student of Emanuel Bach, most of the serious German-language writing on music appeared in the northern and middle regions, with centers in Berlin, Hamburg and Leipzig (not in Vienna). Consequently, while there is relatively little theory or criticism that deals directly with music of the emerging Viennese Classical style, there is a good deal of writing whose point of reference is the music of the North German composers. Much of this writing is directly related to the Berlin circle of composers centered around Sebastian and Emanuel Bach and their students. One might mention treatises by Nichelmann, Kirnberger and Emanuel himself, as well as those of Marpurg. To these one might add the writings of Mattheson and Scheibe, which indicate the general currents of musical thought in Germany during Emanuel Bach's youth, and those of Forkel and Koch, who, though of a later generation, refer occasionally to Bach's music and continue to express ideas more closely associated with the North German style than with any other, particularly in their earlier works.

The subjects of these writings can be divided for convenience into two categories: aesthetics and criticism, and the craft of composition. Criticism often is vague, merely a characterization for the lay reader of a work's tone or level of sophistication. Yet, while of limited value as a source of analytic ideas in individual works, the more philosophical of the critical writings help define one perspective from which the style may be judged: its degree of success in meeting the expressive aspirations of the age. Bach's *improvisations,* at least, seem to have been highly successful, as Burney's admiring account of one session at the clavichord shows.[1] Burney's oft-quoted description of Bach's performance seems to illustrate the composer's exemplification of his own dictum that "a musician cannot move others unless he too is moved."[2] Yet the importance which Burney and Bach himself seem to attach to direct emotional expression in performance should not be exaggerated in considering the role such expression plays in Bach's compositions. Certainly emotional expression became the chief concern in the musical aesthetic of Bach's younger colleagues. Mattheson, a chief spokesman for an earlier generation, had still regarded expression as secondary: music's purpose for him was, "after the praise of God, to delight and move the listener."[3] But with Forkel the single point of music is clearly to preserve (*erhalten*) an "emotional feeling from a certain point in experience."[4] Indeed, Forkel and his contemporaries frequently speak of musical *Ideen, Bildern, Meinungen,* and other concrete entities as though they were intrinsic and essential to music. Music for them becomes a metaphor with a quite specific emotional or programmatic referent.

The idea of music as metaphor is already explicit in Scheibe, whose famous criticism of Sebastian Bach's music was based on that composer's use of dark and turgid "musical metaphors" (*musicalische Metaphora*) whose meaning Scheibe found obscure.[5] For Scheibe these metaphors evidently took the form of discrete musical figures, that is, the "embellished expressions" (*verblühmte Ausdrucken*) described below as the fundamental units of melody in the music of both Sebastian and Emanuel Bach. Thus Scheibe's complaints about the music of the elder Bach went to the heart of his style as well as his teaching of composition, which Scheibe himself had studied with the master; they were not based merely on the accusation that the performer's license to improvise embellishments had been appropriated by the composer.

The same view of music as explicit metaphor lies beneath eighteenth-century hermeneutic interpretations of Emanuel's music, a category which includes not only the narrative programs furnished by Cramer for several pieces,[6] but also the more abstract *Recensionen* of Forkel, which depend on the latter's view of the sonata as a musical corrolary of the strophic ode.[7] Closely related to this attitude was that of the poet Gerstenberg, who provided two texts for Bach's keyboard fantasia H. 75/3 (*W. 63/6/3*).[8] Helm suggests viewing the texted versions of the fantasia "not as a song with an elaborate accompaniment, but a keyboard fantasia containing its own verbal exegesis; the voice is literalizing the meaning of the music."[9] Perhaps it would be better to say that the structure and material of the music (not its "meaning") find a running parallel, at least at the syntactic or grammatical level, in the poetic texts. The existence of *two* texts, one a version of Hamlet's soliloquy, the other a monolog of Socrates as he drinks the hemlock, illustrates—besides Gerstenberg's exalted view of the piece—how the same music might represent two different dramatic situations. In fact, Gerstenberg's texts seem to be an answer to his own complaint that music without words "only treats of general ideas."[10] Gerstenberg—like Berlioz and other Romantics—required music to represent *something*, even if the object represented was not specified by the music itself.

There is good reason to believe that Bach himself harbored similar thoughts, at least on occasion. Lessing quoted him as praising Georg Philip Telemann as "a great depicter [*ein grosser Mahler*]," noting the older composer's ability in a certain aria to express himself so clearly that the text is unnecessary to convey its meaning. But Lessing goes on to cite Bach's criticism of occasional excesses in Telemann's "imitation" (*Nachahmung*), as when "he paints things which music hardly should be supposed to depict."[11] Thus, while taste permitted various degrees of "imitation," there is little reason to doubt that Bach accepted the underlying assumption of musical representation along with the rest of his social and artistic circle.[12]

Modern writers have injected some confusion into the matter by supposing that there is an essential difference between an older "representational" means of expression and newer types of expression which are somehow more direct. At the same time they disagree as to which type of expression Bach uses. Arnold Schering, describing Bach's expression as a *redende Prinzip*, favors the "older" type in Bach. He insists that, for the eighteenth century, musical expression required the evocation of specific, concrete affects.[13] Berg, too, takes Bach's use of certain Baroque affective conventions as "relics" of an older representational system of expression (and therefore, in her terms, evidence of mannerism).[14] On the other hand, Beurmann finds that in slow movements "the affect is no longer symbol but achieves actuality."[15] Manfred Bukofzer, though not specifically concerned with Emanuel Bach, posits a similar change in the means of musical expression, which he places in roughly the period in which Bach achieved artistic maturity. Bukofzer claims that "Baroque music is not, like modern music, a language of feeling, which expresses its objects directly, but a sort of indirect iconology in sound." This is to buttress his contention that Baroque "allegory" is "non-expressive, non-psychological in character."[16] Yet this theory depends on the assumption that the "symbolic" means of expression employed (to the exclusion of others?) in the Baroque was, or is, perceived differently from what

Bukofzer regards as the unmediated emotional expression of later music. Long crescendos or decrescendos, prolonged or accented dissonances, and similar effects more characteristic of Romantic than of eighteenth-century music still depend on the listener's perception and understanding of such musical signs as the prolonged dissonance. The latter can represent—or produce—a state of heightened emotional tension only for a listener who knows that it implies a forthcoming release of tension, indicated by another specific musical sign (in this case, the resolution of the dissonance). Such signs do not seem to be fundamentally different from those of the Baroque; the music is still tonal. But in Baroque music the signs having emotional significance tend to be concise motives—hence their emblematic qualities—while in later music an extended crescendo or a prolonged dissonance (with its resolution) constitutes a *process* operating over a much wider span of music. In Schenkerian terms, expressivity is located further—not necessarily much further—toward the background.

The deep emotional impression which Bach's music and his own performances made on his contemporaries no doubt played some small role in the early history of musical and literary Romanticism. But there are suggestions that Bach's own preference was not to emphasize the expressive aspect of his own work at the expense of the purely musical. Neither Emanuel nor his younger brother Friedrich, in replies to letters from Gerstenberg, encourages the poet's view of their music as expressing concrete programmatic *Ideen*.[17] While Emanuel does make frequent reference in the *Versuch* to expressive conventions or to the affectual significance of various ornaments and other musical devices, the expression of emotion in Emanuel's music runs deeper than the simple associations that might be summarized in a *Verzeichnis der Affekte*.[18] Such expression, however, is inseparable from the formal aspects of the music. Even the large-scale design of a composition represents the fulfillment of some expressive aspiration and symbolizes some aesthetic position, though the expressive function of a form is less easily identified than the "affect" associated by convention with certain local devices. Forkel's comparison between the sonata and the ode, or his cataloguing of musico-rhetorical devices. perhaps provides a hint to how his contemporaries would have articulated the relationship between musical and literary expression. But to consider the matter in such terms is only to draw analogies. A fuller discussion of what Emanuel Bach's music might express demands nothing less than a thorough stylistic analysis of the works themselves, in terms derived from but not bound by contemporary theory on the art of composition.

The theoretical sources consist chiefly of treatises on composition or performance: practical introductions to the techniques which a musician was expected to master and employ in his own works. Both types of treatise share two concerns of fundamental interest to this study: a sensitivity to local rhythm and articulation, which upon extension to larger rhythmic units leads to considerations of musical form; and an interest in embellishment and what is called "variation" as the source of material, that is, the musical surface.

As a general expression for the ornamentation or alteration of existing material, "variation" is a useful term for the technique used to provide Bach's sonata movements with varied reprises and in general to relieve the sameness of recurring melodic material. But in a more specific sense variation can be understood as part of the process of producing an original work. The term *Veränderung* is not always used in this more specific sense in the theoretical sources, but it is a convenient expression under which to unite various references to what seems to have been a conventional North German conception of improvisation and composition.

The most famous illustration of this technique is in the closing chapter of Bach's *Versuch*, where the composer reveals his method of improvising a free fantasia. He begins with a figured bass line, which he terms a framework (*Gerippe*), and upon it constructs the little keyboard Fantasia H. 160 (W. *117/14*). Schenker's study of this chapter claims "to present an unpretentious contribution to the art of diminution, which is the principal medium of the free fantasia."[19] Indeed, Schenker takes composition itself, at least in the works of an eighteenth-century composer like Bach, as being none other than "the art of diminution, the auskomponierung [sic] of chords."[20] Schenker's interpretation of Bach's "diminution technique" in terms of his own analytic method is open to question. But there is ample evidence in the eighteenth-century theorists, apart from Bach himself, that some sort of diminution or variation was understood as a basic compositional technique, at least at what Schenker would regard as the surface of the music.

The earliest explicit discussion of this technique, and perhaps the source of the term *Veränderung* in the sense in which I am using it, may be found in Friedrich Erhard Niedt's *Handleitung zur Variation*, published at Hamburg in 1706. In this work, Niedt demonstrates the technique by presenting a figured bass line and its "realization" in each of the movements of a keyboard suite.[21] In contrast to similar works by earlier composers, such as the Suite "auff die Mayerin" by Froberger, Niedt's suite is derived from an original bass line which, incidentally, generates a prototype of the ternary sonata form described later in this chapter. While composers had been writing sets of variations on ground basses for well over a century, and theorists had been describing the techniques of improvising over short repeated bass lines for at least as long, it was only with Niedt, apparently, that the composition of original, independent pieces was described as the "variation" of a harmonic/contrapuntal *Satz* represented by a figured bass. Like earlier writers, Niedt understood melodies as being composed of chains of short figures—which, like his predecessors, he categorizes with scholastic zeal. Beginning with Niedt, however, the melodic figures are understood as the composing-out of harmonies, not as refinements or embellishments used in setting a line of counterpoint against a cantus firmus. Niedt's formulation made it possible to distinguish what we would call motives from the many other types of musico-rhetorical figures. No longer was composition simply the equivalent of counterpoint; the species of variation could be described separately from those of counterpoint (and of musical rhetoric), as the organization of Niedt's treatise and subsequent German writings shows.

The technique of composition—or improvisation—through "variation" lies beneath the exercises in the *Gross General-Bass-Schule* of Mattheson, who had edited and published the third, posthumous, volume of Niedt's treatise.[22] Its most thorough demonstration, however, is in Sebastian Bach's Goldberg Variations, published in 1741, which illustrate (among other things) the applicability of this manner of composing to all of the genres and styles, both strict and *galant,* in which Sebastian could imagine writing. Indeed, the Goldberg Variations are indirect evidence that the doctrine of composition as variation was, as I suggested earlier, central to Sebastian Bach's teaching of composition. This is suggested not only by Scheibe but by descriptions of Sebastian's pedagogy stemming from both Kirnberger and Emanuel Bach. Evidently the elder Bach skipped species counterpoint and commenced the teaching to composition with four-part figured bass realization—a necessary first step prior to "variation."[23]

A related document from the Bach circle is Kirnberger's curious "Method for Tossing Off Sonatas," as Newman renders it.[24] The method begins by taking a pre-existing "sonata"—that is, any instrumental work in two voices— and first replacing its bass line with a new one, then writing a new treble (or vice versa). Kirnberger illustrates the technique by applying it to the Gigue in Sebastian Bach's sixth French Suite.[25]

The significance of Kirnberger's "method" was recognized by Newman, who saw in it

> two main tenets that reappear throughout Kirnberger's writings . . . One is that counterpoint originates in figurate harmony (as in Bach's four-part chorale harmonizations) and the other is that melody originates in the realization of thoroughbass (which is not quite the same as Rameau's idea that "melody is born of harmony").[26]

Elsewhere Kirnberger himself writes that

> in music today the most important part is the bass, which subordinates all the [upper] voices. When the composer has correctly selected the series of bass notes and properly set the upper voices, then the composition is pure.[27]

The "Art of Pure Composition" (*Kunst des reinen Satzes*) is, of course, the subject of Kirnberger's principal work, in which composition is regarded as beginning with a figured bass and its more or less elaborate realization. What

Kirnberger calls "florid, colorful melody" (*verziehŕte, bunte Gesang*) is produced by varying the tones of the underlying harmonies through arpeggiation (*Brechung*) or passing tones (*durchgehende Töne*). *Brechung*, for example, is defined as when "the tones serving as embellishment are taken from the underlying harmony."[28] Various sorts of *Brechung* are then illustrated, among them several examples incorporating non-chord tones (*acciaccature*). The latter sort of arpeggiation is especially frequent in Bach's music:

Ex. 3-1.   a)   J.P. Kirnberger, illustrations of arpeggiation
incorporating non-harmonic tones (marked by
asterisks), from *Die Kunst des reinen Satzes,* vol. 1
(Berlin, 1771), p. 217.

b)   C.P.E. Bach, *Variationes mit veränderten Reprisen.*
H. 259 (*W. 118/10*) 105-8.

Kirnberger's discussion spells out the details of the compositional method that Scheibe had alluded to many years earlier:

It is understood that no melody is beautiful that lacks certain variations of the main notes, certain additions, diminutions, expansions, and other subtle embellishments almost continuously.... [An embellished musical expression] is in fact a new and pleasing variation of a short melodic idea in order to make the latter more impressive, or even more sublime, without departing from the harmony.[29]

In Scheibe's account it is not yet clear that the melody actually proceeds from the harmony; he only suggests that the "embellished musical expressions" (*verblühmte Ausdrucken*) must not clash with the underlying chord. Scheibe's term *verblühmte Ausdruck* is difficult to translate; evidently it refers to a discrete motive or figure, like one of Kirnberger's *Ausziehrungen*. As such it is distinct from another type of "figure," the rhetorical type, which will be discussed shortly.[30]

Marpurg, like Scheibe, distinguishes between rhetorical figures and what he calls *Setzmanieren* or *figures de composition*.[31] Marpurg's figures of composition were discussed by Beurmann in connection with Bach's *Reprisen-Sonaten*, presumably because at one point Marpurg does refer to the figures as "variations."[32] But there is no reason to think that Marpurg meant that the *Setzmanieren* were used only in variations in the modern sense. Like Kirnberger's *Ausziehrungen*, Marpurg's figures of composition are the basic material of any melodic line, falling into categories comparable to the types of *Ausziehrungen* described and illustrated by Kirnberger.

Veränderung is an important concern in Emanuel Bach's compositions. Beside the *Sechs Sonaten mit veränderte Reprisen* (the *Reprisen-Sonaten*, W. 50), there are a number of pieces which *NV* describes as having undergone variation to produce alternate versions. Among these is the Sonata H. 150 (W. *51/1*), which was "afterwards varied twice throughout" to produce the Sonatas H. 156 and 157 (*W. 65/35, 36*).[33] A manuscript collection of *Veränderungen und Auszierungen über einige gedruckten Sonaten für Scholaren*, H. 164 (*W. 68*), includes not only varied reprises for a number of works published without them, but embellished versions of a number of through-composed movements.[34] There are also many published works, in addition to the *Reprisen-Sonaten*, containing varied reprises, as well as frequent instances of variation technique in other pieces, especially the Sonatines and Rondos. In the case of H. 156 and 157 the compositional procedure involved the rewriting of an entire three-movement sonata at the level of the musical surface; form, rhythm, and harmonic progression were naturally unaltered. Quite the same procedure was employed in revising some of the early sonatas, for example in the slow movements of H. 16 and 18 (*W. 65/7 and 9*).[35] Similar types of revision occurred in later works as well, usually to incorporate more elaborate embellishment or more active passage-work.[36]

Thus "variation" involves more than the altered repetition of previously heard material. Some of Bach's embellishments, such as those in the autograph score of the slow movement of the Concerto H. 441 (*W. 31*), recall the performing tradition of embellishing the slow movements of sonatas and concertos, a practice described by Quantz, among others.[37] But the rewriting of solo passage-work in the quick movements of a concerto or of the opening theme in a sonata goes beyond anything that might be considered improvisatory in the strict sense. For that matter, even the varied reprises of W. 50, intended as models for improvisation, have crystallized into something far more formal and stylized than one would expect in genuinely improvised ornamentation, if only because the same embellishments are almost always used when material heard at one part of the sonata form returns later.[38] The roots of "variation" must lie in the ancient practice of improvised embellishment, as Bach implies by discussing varied reprises in the chapter of the *Versuch* which deals with performance in general.[39] But for Bach and his North German colleagues variation, in the sense used here, seems to have been the principal means of converting an abstract harmonic progression, in the form of a figured bass, into an individual composition. As Chapter 4 will argue, Bach's reliance on this technique has important consequences for the nature of his melodic material and its relationship to the work as a whole.

Beside variation, which is essentially the invention of melodic material, the treatises are frequently concerned with rhythm, phrasing and form, matters usually discussed within the context of musical rhetoric. Indeed, one might argue that the greatest value of eighteenth-century musical rhetoric (*Klangrede*) lay in the impetus it gave toward the development of theories of musical form and rhythm, and not in its occasional use as a form of hermeneutics, or to illustrate analogies between music and other arts. As has already been noted, a number of writers take pains to distinguish between melodic figures and the figures of rhetoric. Marpurg mentions that the "figures" can be used to express a certain affect or situation, but by "figure" he refers to the use of a given motive or melodic idea for expressive purposes, not the motive itself.[40] Scheibe, in a passage quoted by Berg, describes the figure *ellipsis* (*Verbeisen*) as "when one unexpectedly breaks off at the most passionate affect in the middle of a phrase and comes to a complete stop, but then begins anew with a completely different idea."[41] *Ellipsis* thus refers to the practice of juxtaposing two contrasting types of music; the term describes the syntactic relationship between two musical passages without referring to the specific material of either.

To be sure, certain musical motives are often employed in ways that correspond to some of the rhetorical figures as catalogued by theorists of *Klangrede*, so that the distinction between musical and rhetorical figures may at times be somewhat academic. Thus Berg refers to a Baroque affective *motif*, the descending chromatic bass used by Bach in the Sonata H. 119 (*W. 62/19*)3, as a rhetorical figure.[42] But the most interesting conclusions that can be drawn from *Klangrede* involve not the association of single musical motives with particular rhetorical devices, but rather the similar structures and rhythms of musical and verbal expression. For example, the elegance of eighteenth-century prose has a direct parallel in *galant* music, particularly in the use of an intricate hierarchy of local articulations, creating the possibility of subtle and complex nuances and parentheses within single phrases. An understanding of musical rhetoric is therefore of some use in performing eighteenth-century music; the rhetorical qualities of the music can be expressed by observing its detailed articulation into brief figures, each of which may itself fall into separate groups of slurred and detached notes.

What might be called the rhetorical style—an expression preferable to the somewhat pejorative *zerhackte*[43]—is especially important in Bach's Berlin chamber music, and on one occasion leads to a programmatic work exploiting the obvious implications of some of the rhetorical figures. Berg notes the similarity of Scheibe's *Interrogatio* to the question (*Frage*) described in Bach's exegetical preface to the *Programm-Trio* H. 580 (*W. 161/1*).[44] But modern descriptions have over-emphasized the programmatic nature of this work, which dates from 1749 and therefore precedes by some two decades the programs provided for works of Bach by Cramer and others. Bach's "program" here is limited to abstract analogies to rhetoric and conversation. The rhythmic-motivic relationships described in the preface in terms of a disagreement and subsequent reconciliation are employed throughout Bach's music, if rarely with such concentration on the more extreme rhetorical effects (such as *ellipsis*).

The theorists' analogy to rhetoric is usually confined to discussions of local events, although Mattheson and Forkel continue the analogy to the point of analyzing whole movements, and even cycles, in terms of a classical oration.[45] In fact, Mattheson's rhetorical conception of form somewhat resembles that of the nineteenth century, since it is based on an *Inventio* or *Haupterfindung*, that is, a theme in the literal sense, which is developed or expounded upon in the course of the work. But the strictly rhetorical conception of form is overshadowed in Marpurg, Koch and others by a conception of form as a combination of tonal and rhythmic effects.[46] Thus Koch and Marpurg present their theories of harmony and modulation prior to any discussion of form, including the latter in subsequent treatments of rhythm and phrasing. Even so, in describing musical structure both writers continue to rely heavily on purely rhythmic concepts derived from rhetoric and poetics, especially at the more local levels. Thus Marpurg develops a set of terms for the hierarchy of rhythmic levels in a piece, building from the *Rhythmus* up to the *Period* or *Paragraph*.[47] Koch later criticized the confusing proliferation of such terms in writers after Marpurg; Koch's rhythmic hierarchy is limited to the *Einschnitt, Absatz* (or *Satz*) and *Period*, although he uses the first two of these terms somewhat loosely.[48]

Whatever their precise meaning in a given musical context, these terms are of primarily rhythmic significance in that they refer only to the relative duration of a passage or section of a work, not at all to its motivic content or structural function. Thus none of the terms corresponds exactly to the modern "motive"; the *Einschnitt*, the smallest articulation in Koch's system, is a brief portion of music which does not express a complete "idea" (*Gedanken*), that is, a complete phrase. At the largest level, a piece is viewed as being composed of two or three functionally identical *Perioden*, distinguished only in terms of the key of the final cadence in each and not according to the expository, developmental, or recapitulatory function of the section. Actually the therorists are not entirely unaware of structural functions for certain important passages. Koch distinguishes the *Schlussabsatz*, the last phrase of a period, from the other *Absätze*; he likewise recognizes an opening phrase as a *Thema* or *Hauptsatz*. Yet Koch is not interested in the melodic material of the theme or its development; he is content to note the possibility of repeating the opening idea at the head of subsequent periods, or of recapitulating the closing portion of the initial period at the end of the last one.[49]

In its codification of the various instrumental and vocal forms, Koch's *Versuch* is a culmination of the tendencies of earlier North German theorists. Koch views all of the larger forms essentially as expansions of what Rosen has called two- and three-period types of simple binary form.[50] Hence Koch really has only a single harmonically conceived sonata form for all instrumental pieces, with alternate two- and three-section versions. Newman, as well as other writers, has made much of the existence of binary and ternary versions of sonata form in the eighteenth century.[51] LaRue even posits seven hypothetical steps in the "functional evolution of sonata form" from Baroque binary form to the mature Classical sonata-allegro.[52] But the basic binary and ternary forms are already present in early works of the North German school, as in the outer movements of Bach's Sonata H. 16 (*W. 65/7*), dating (in its original version) from 1736. For that matter, full-fledged binary and ternary forms, meeting all the criteria suggested by Marpurg's, if not Koch's, discussions of musical structure, are common enough in the late Baroque works of Händel, Telemann, and J.S. Bach.

To a remarkable extent, sonatas from throughout Bach's career illustrate the relatively simple, unarticulated form described by the theorists. This is to say that they lack clear functional distinctions between the two or three *Hauptperioden*, clearly articulated primary and secondary tonal areas, and other elements of Classical sonata-form which are common knowledge to modern writers but unrecognized by the eighteenth-century theorists.

In one respect Emanuel Bach routinely goes beyond the very simple sonata form described by Marpurg. This is in his tendency to include a retransition, which occurs in a three-part form as a modulating passage between the cadence at the end or the second section and the return of the principal theme at the beginning of the third. Koch speaks of the retransition as an appendage (*Anhang*) to the second *Period*[53]—thus clarifying a point which was not entirely satisfactory in Marpurg's analysis of a piece attributed to

Emanuel Bach.[54] But even Koch, whose familiarity with the Classical style is suggested by several quotations from Haydn in the *Versuch,*[55] maintains the same basic conception of form as Marpurg or even Scheibe. While he has some sense of the special character of the central *Period* in a ternary movement, or of thematic parallelism between the opening and closing sections, neither is crucial to the form in Koch's view. Observations of this sort have led one writer on eighteenth-century form to comment that any reference to a "shortened recapitulation" (*verkürtzer Reprise*) or to an "underelaborated development" (*unterentwickelter Durchführung*) is inappropriate.[56] Indeed, to use any of the three modern terms for the three main sections of most Bach sonata movements is to risk raising unjustified expectations. As the theorists would suggest, the functions of exposition, development and recapitulation, as generally understood today, are only weakly differentiated in the North German ternary form, even less so in binary form. For this reason the following chapters avoid the modern terms, sticking with the more awkward but less misleading "parts" or "sections" to refer to the *Perioden* of the theorists. It will be useful, however, to retain the terms "retransition" and "return," since these refer to specific types of passage undeniably present in many works. ("Return" will refer to any passage in which opening material returns in the tonic.)

If reference to the theorists can help simplify the discussion of sonata movements, the same is true in other types of movement derived from the basic form, notably in concertos. As Stevens's article points out, the "primary structure of the movement" in Koch's version of concerto form lies with the solo passages. These, not the tutti sections, constitute the *Hauptperioden* presenting what Koch calls the "course of modulation" (*Gang der Modulation*).[57] Koch's description calls for three *Hauptperioden* in a concerto movement, but many of Bach's seem to present four equally important solo sections. Indeed, Riepel had earlier described the concerto in terms of either three or four *Hauptsolo*; in describing an "extremely long" (*überaus lang*) movement with four solos, Riepel seems to draw an important distinction between the concerto and the ternary sonata or symphony.[58]

If Riepel's understanding of the mid-century concerto is correct, it would seem to cast doubt on Koch's value as an observer of form for this period, especially since his view of concerto form is based on "principally the harpsichord concertos of Carl Philipp Emanuel Bach," according to Stevens.[59] This point is open to question. What Koch says is that many of Bach's concerti illustrate an ideal drawn from the opposition of solo and chorus in classical tragedy[60]—more a statement about aesthetics than form. The remark is part of a defense of the concerto against criticisms of the form in the *Allgemeine Theorie* of Sulzer; Koch's reply is that a concerto can be no less expressive than an aria.[61] In fact, Koch's concerto form resembles that of an aria in its use of formally inessential *ritornelli*, the chief difference between the two forms being the incorporation of passage-work (*Passagen*) into the principal *Perioden*, that is, the solos, of a concerto.

As Chapter 6 will demonstrate, the distinctions between the three-, four-, and even five-tutti forms mentioned by modern writers are inconsequential for most of Bach's concertos. For that matter, it seems wrong to employ terms based on the number of ritornellos;[62] to do so is to attract attention to the frame rather than the substance of the pre-Classical concerto. The frame may be rather ornate in later examples; still, composers like Emanuel Bach never abandoned the close structural and aesthetic relationship between concerto movement and aria. Hence the description of the form given by Koch, with its three main sections, can always be adapted to Bach's mature concerto movements. The source of the confusion is that most of Bach's concerto movements include a passage functioning as retransition; this is played by the soloist in some works, by the tutti in others. Such a passage is neither ritornello nor solo in a structural sense, although in form and proportions it often approaches the other sections of the movement, creating a structural ambiguity which Koch evidently chose to ignore in the *Versuch*.[63]

Despite such inadequacies, the writings discussed in this chapter furnish a rudimentary vocabulary for the criticism and analysis of Bach's music while bringing to light elements in the music that might be overlooked, or whose importance might be under-estimated, by the modern listener. In general, they emphasize the role of elegant detail, in both the "variation" incorporated into every melody and the subtle, precise articulation required to render clearly the numerous small rhythmic divisions of every piece. Relatively little attention is paid to the subtleties of large-scale form or motivic relationships. This is what might be expected in writers who seem to adopt whole-heartedly the manneristic North German style. On the other hand, the theorists' occasional loss for words cannot justify our own. Haydn himself may have had no better language than Koch's to describe his own works, which nevertheless manifest a far deeper awareness of the possibilities of eighteenth-century style. Surely the same is true, at least sometimes, of Emanuel Bach.

4

Texture and Material

The fundamental language of Emanuel Bach's music does not differ in essentials from that of his contemporaries, despite the eccentricities in which certain of his works abound. His textures, forms, and means of composing a melodic line are those found in the music of other composers of his generation and taught in the treatises of Kirnberger, Koch, and others. Thus a systematic stylistic analysis of Emanuel's instrumental music will contain a good deal that is relevant to the music of his contemporaries as well, especially those composers who remained within the sphere of the "North German mannerists." Yet the very consistency with which Emanuel Bach applied certain principles is a special characteristic of his music, distinguishing it from that of his older brother Friedemann, which tends to be more flexible in formal matters, as well as that of his younger brother Friedrich, which hints at a greater acceptance of the more southerly "comic" style. Emanuel's music underwent neither the radical change in style which Christian's did under the influence of Italian opera, nor did it evolve gradually toward a less manneristic style, as did Haydn's. Hence it is possible to speak of a single style in the music of Emanuel Bach, embracing virtually all of the works of his adult life, from the late 1730's to 1788.

For the most part the texture of Bach's music follows principles carried over from his father's music and that of other late Baroque composers, especially Vivaldi and other Italians. The music is conceived almost entirely in *obligato* contrapuntal lines; instrumentation is of secondary importance except, of course, in the keyboard music, where one finds the predictable types of figuration and *Freistimmigkeit*. Even here, however, the *choice* of keyboard instrument is not always clear. The addition or amplification of the dynamic markings in Bach's Berlin revisions of early keyboard sonatas suggests that by the 1740's he had adopted the clavichord as the preferred medium for his solo works, as comments scattered throughout the *Versuch* and Burney's description of his playing also suggest. Yet in the autographs of the keyboard concertos and trios, Bach retains (as did Mozart) the designation *cembalo*. While harpsichord is not impossible in any of these works, it is essential in only one—the Double-Concerto for harpsichord and fortepiano, H. 479 (*W. 47*), one of Bach's last works—and most of the works written after 1750 or so are probably more effective on fortepiano. Harpsichord *is* impossible in the late solo works, such as those in the collections *für Kenner und Liebhaber,* which demand fluid dynamics and, in several instances, the so-called *Bebung* or vibrato possible only on the clavichord.

Yet the basic texture of the keyboard music varies little; apart from the more detailed notation of dynamics, the keyboard idiom in the late works remains close to that of the 1730's and '40's. The same is true of Bach's ensemble music. As in most eighteenth-century instrumental music—Sebastian Bach's excluded—the number of real contrapuntal parts is rarely more than two or three; even in orchestral music four (or more) parts is a rarity, with the violins more often playing in unison or the violas doubling the bass, which Bach writes as a fully figured continuo part even in his very last works. Except in a few special sets from the Hamburg period, the wind parts in the symphonies and concertos are optional and inessential, in many cases added long after the original composition—a practice which Emanuel applied to the works of other composers as well, in keeping with eighteenth-century tradition. Also characteristic of the century is the existence of alternate versions, for varying instruments, of certain trio-sonatas and concertos, and the uncertainty regarding the intended instrument for much of the keyboard music, despite the clear preference which Emanuel expressed for the clavichord in solo playing.

The simplification of Baroque counterpoint is, of course, one of the marks of the *galant* manner which Emanuel's generation embraced with few reservations. Individual phrases of a trio sonata, keyboard sonata, or orchestral work may introduce imitations or otherwise expand the number of real voices beyond the usual two or three. But the upper parts in such cases rarely achieve significant rhythmic or melodic independence; hence the frequency of the "canonic" sequence, which is more antiphonal than genuinely contrapuntal. (Ex. 4-1)

Thus even in the trio-sonatas and other ostensibly polyphonic works, Bach's basic texture is a single leading line set over a figured or unfigured bass. The bass is the only essential accompanying part; one finds little of the rich variety of accompaniment idioms characteristic of the Classical style, either the Alberti type of arpeggiation in keyboard music or the various idiomatic varieties of accompaniment possible in ensemble music. Moreover, the basic texture of a movement, once established, remains constant; the chief source of variety lies in the character of the figuration or embellishment of the principal voices.

In this predominantly two-part texture, the bass line is quite as important in establishing the character of a piece as it is in the Baroque style. But although a few works have a bass as florid as the treble (e.g., the sonata movements H. 281 (W. *59/1*)2 and H. 287 (W. *61/5*)3), the bass is usually limited to the repeated notes, "walking" lines, and other familiar techniques of early

Ex. 4-1.   Trio-sonata *(Programm-Trio)* in C minor for two violins
and continuo (1749), H. 579 *(W. 161/1)* 3/142-48.

eighteenth-century basses. Hence the outer parts are sharply differentiated—a
florid, variegated treble set against a simpler, more regular bass. The result is a
texture resembling that of a Baroque solo sonata: Newman's "melo/bass"
texture.[1] This sort of texture is frequent even in the keyboard sonatas, where
entire movements continue to be written in two parts, as in many Baroque
keyboard works, though usually without the contrapuntal interplay typical of
the latter. When Bach does aim at genuine polyphony, the result may be

somewhat self-conscious, as in the last movement of the sixth Württemberg sonata, H. 36 (*W. 49/6*), an exercise in double-counterpoint which stands in severe contrast to the galant texture of the two heavily *empfindsam* movements that precede it.

Except in such pieces Bach's bass lines rarely contain anything of thematic interest. They tend rather to preserve cadential formulas and rhythmic patterns reminiscent of Baroque bass lines. Hence Bach's harmonic rhythm and pacing remain close to those of the 1720's, though absolute tempos may have slowed somewhat under heavy embellishment of the upper line. Even under an ornate, rhetorical, treble line, the bass is likely to remain relatively simple, maintaining a Baroque linear continuity in the freest keyboard fantasias and rondos. Bach's attachment to certain simple bass formulas as foundation for opening thematic statements, though shared with his contempoaries, is noteworthy for the variety of ways in which both the bass itself and the upper part are subjected to "variation" in works dating from throughout his career. Perhaps the most common of these recurring bass lines is a simple diationic descent, as in the Sonata H. 187 (*W. 55/6*), where such a bass underlies both the opening and closing themes of the first movement.

Ex. 4-2.   Sonata in G (1765), H. 187 *(W. 55/6).*
　　　　　a)   1/1-3.

　　　b)   1/20-22.

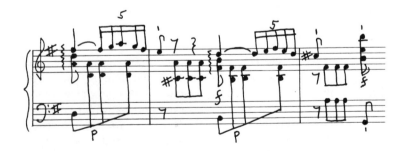

The same bass can occur with certain tones displaced rhythmically; note in particular the delay of the third note and the subsequent deceleration of the harmonic rhythm in the following example, taken from one of Bach's more manneristic works:

Ex. 4-3.   Sonata in C (1775), H. 248 *(W. 65/47)* 1/1-6.

Such an example is easier to understand when analyzed through reduction to a figured bass, which indicates not only the essential tones "varied" in the musical surface, but also, by retaining definite note values, the harmonic rhythm of the original.

Ex. 4-4.   Figured bass sketch for Ex. 3. The slur indicates arpeggiation of a single harmony.

To be sure, not all passages in Bach's music are constructed over descending scale-segments. Nor is Emanuel Bach the only composer ever to have combined a florid upper line with a simple underlying progression. What is to be observed here, however, is the consistent combination of a rhythmically complex or fragmented melodic line with a relatively simple linear foundation. Long passages may be built over linear basses encompassing two, three, or more descents through a full octave. In the following example virtually half of the second solo section of a concerto movement is built over a continuously descending bass.

Ex. 4-5.   Concerto in D minor (1745), H. 420 *(W. 17)* 1/83-96, cembalo part only.

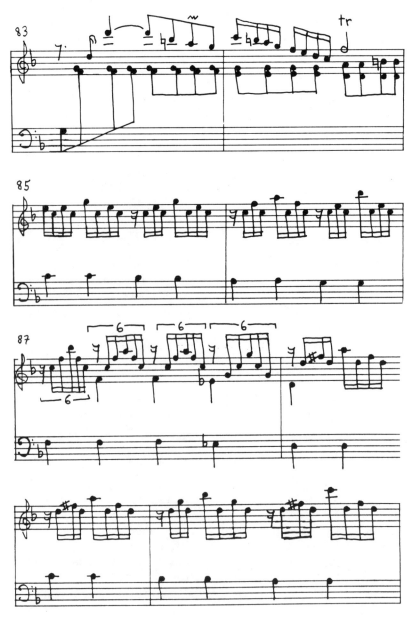

Ex. 4-5. (continued)

An unusual development of this idea occurs in the A-major Fantasia, H. 278 (*W. 58/6*).

Ex. 4-6.   Fantasia in A (1782), H. 278 *(W. 58/7),* first section
(unbarred.)

As in the preceding examples, the diversity of the surface masks the relatively simple linearity of the underlying *Satz:*

Ex. 4-7.   Figured bass sketch of Ex. 6.

The shifting register of the bass, the chromatic and enharmonic intervals in all voices, as well as the performer's rhythmic freedom (symbolized by the absence of bar-lines and the changing tempo markings) all create tensions against the simple downward movement of the basic line.

In an extraordinary passage from the Rondo in A minor, H. 262 (*W. 56/5*), a similar chromatic descent in the bass combines with a rising chromatic line in the treble.

Ex. 4-8.   Rondo in A minor (1778), H. 262 *(W. 56/5)*.
            a)   Mm. 142-57.

Ex. 4-8.   (continued)

b)   Sketch of mm. 142-55.

But in this case no lasting modulation occurs; the entire chromatic passage is embedded within a statement of the four-measure rondo theme, a characteristic harmonic parenthesis of a sort discussed more fully in Chapter 6.

Bach's use of linear basses is related to his frequent reliance on sequence. Sequences are essentially elaborations of linear progressions; their prevalence in Bach's music, as in earlier Baroque music, is not surprising, though Bach is perhaps more inclined than his predecessors to employ sequences in opening themes (as in Example 4-2a). One of Bach's favorite sequential basses is of

Ex. 4-9. a) Piano trio in A minor (1775), H. 552 *(W. 90/1)*
            63-66, violin omitted.

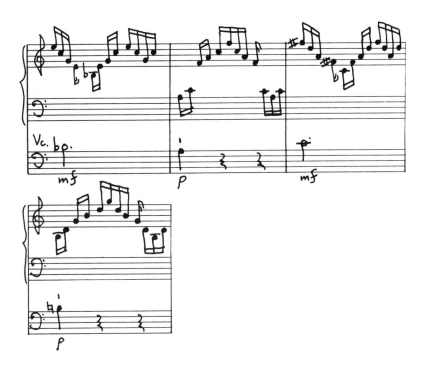

b) Flute concerto in D minor, H. 426 (arrangement of
    W. 22, 1745), 3/75-78, inner parts omitted.

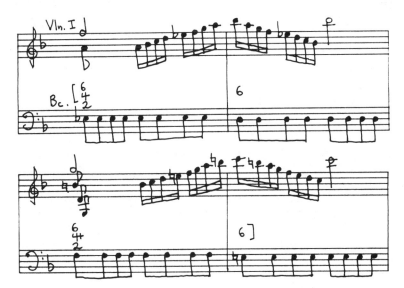

special interest; this is a line based on the motive B-A-C-H, in which the letter H stands, of course, for B-natural. Irving Godt suggested that this idea serves as a signature *motif* in the Symphony H. 660 (*W. 182/3*), which employs it in all three movements.[2] In fact this motive occurs in basses of works written from throughout Bach's career. The motive may be transposed or may lack the characteristic chromaticism, but in either case it is used to ascend sequentially through the circle of fifths. The progression depends on the use of the chord of the augmented fourth (6/4#/2) as an unprepared dissonance resolved by the bass. In the two following examples this produces a distinctive coloring immediately recognizable as Emanuel Bach's. (Ex. 4-9b is on p. 41.)

In all of the preceding examples, the simple linearity of the bass contrasts sharply with the fragmentation of the treble. One result is an exaggeration of the polarization of outer voices that characterizes the "melo/bass" texture. While repeated notes or similar devices in the bass line may somewhat reduce the polarization, in some late works Bach emphasizes the effect by setting rapid treble figuration against bare half- or whole-notes in the bass. (Ex. 4-10)

Ex. 4-10.   Double-Concerto in E-flat for harpsichord, fortepiano
and orchestra (1788), H. 479 *(W. 47)* 1/7-10, inner
parts omitted.

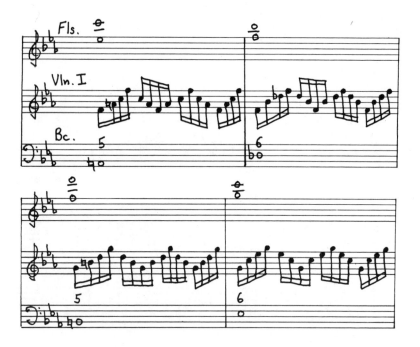

Here the full burden of generating surface motion is cast on the violins. The bass—using a variant of the BACH motive—operates as usual on a broader rhythmic level than the treble; in this case, however, the long sweep of the bass line is communicated to the upper register by the prominent flute parts, which "realize" the bass in long notes floating over the violin arpeggiation.

The last example illustrates the literal application of the theorists' *Brechung* as a source of melodic material. As suggested in Chapter 3, much of the material in Bach's music is generated through such *Brechung* and other sorts of "variation." Naturally it is easiest to demonstrate this where variation—in the modern sense—actually occurred as part of the compositional process, as when a piece exists in more than one version, or when a passage recurs in varied form in the course of a single composition. Berg noted the use of varied repetitions "on many levels of Bach's sonatas,"[3]

Ex. 4-11.   Concerto in E (1744), H. 417 *(W. 14)*.
       a)   1/1-6, inner parts omitted.

    b)   1/213-18.

referring to the employment of variation not only in reprises (varied repetitions) but in the returns of sonata and rondo themes and even in the successive statements of a sequential pattern. What is true of Bach's sonatas is true in other genres as well. The solo sections of the Concerto H. 417 (*W. 14*), first movement, vary the ritornello theme; since the return occurs in the solo part, only the varied form of the theme is heard at the head of the third section. A more subtle case occurs in the flute sonata H. 555 (*W. 127*), where the opening theme of the third movement is immediately varied in measures 5-8. The variation technique here is what Kurt von Fischer calls *Dekolierung*,[4] the

Ex. 4-12.   Sonata in G for flute and continuo (1739), H. 554 *(W. 127)* 3/1-8.

substitution of a slow-moving figure for a more active one. From another point of view measures 5-8 are simply a less active realization of the bass used in measures 1-4. Neither represents the "real" theme, and in the third section the return (such as it is) is recognizable only by the appearance of the *bass* of measures 3-4.[5] (Ex. 4-13)

The most thoroughgoing example of literal variation as a compositional technique occurs in the two "varied" versions of the Sonata H. 150 (*W. 51/1*), as a brief excerpt shows. (Ex. 4-14)

Ex. 4-13.   Same, mm. 63-66.

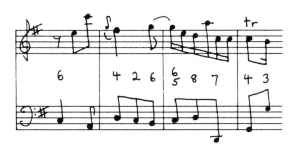

Ex. 4-14.   Sonata in C (1760), H. 150 *(W. 51/1)*, and two varied
             versions, H. 156 *(W 63/35)* and H. 157 *(W. 65/36)*, 3/1-6.

Ex. 4-14.   (continued)

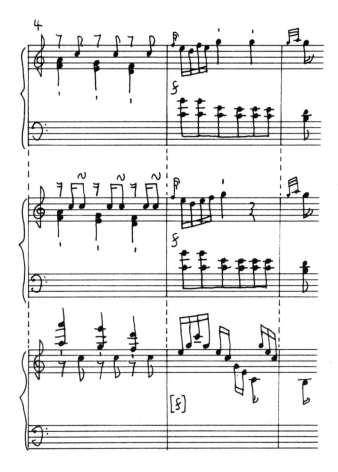

H. 150 and H. 156 stand in a particularly close relationship. Where H. 156 merely presents a figural variation, H. 157 first inverts the original texture (for four measures), then dissolves entirely into arpeggiation. Both of the varied versions, however, maintain almost exactly the same phrasing and foreground voice-leading as the original; it is as though they were intended to show that the melodic surface is irrelevant to the rhythmic and harmonic structure of the piece. Given only H. 156 or 157, one would be hard pressed to ascertain that one was dealing with a "variation" of another work. All three employ similar *types* of material: for the most part, discrete motives or *Setzmanieren* which flesh out the underlying rhythmic and harmonic framework common to the three sonatas.

Many of Bach's revisions in other keyboard sonatas resemble the variations introduced into H. 156 and 157. Indeed, the three concertos H. 430, 434 and 437 (*W. 26, 28* and *29*) present a situation similar to that of H. 150: each exists in alternate versions for flute, cello and harpsichord, the solo part undergoing extensive alteration in each case but with little change in the accompaniments. There are a few slight divergences in the formal ground plan of each concerto, the most important being the expanded second and third sections of the versions for harpsichord and for cello of the Concerto in A, H. 437 (*W. 29*). Wade's conclusions about Bach's revisions are particularly applicable to these works:

> In his [Emanuel Bach's] concertos the bass line, figured or unfigured, played a very important role . . . . Most significantly, the bass line rarely underwent alteration. Generally, when some change in the part-writing became necessary . . . Bach recomposed the three upper parts to accommodate the bass part.[6]

In rewriting the solo parts of certain concertos, Emanuel had a precedent in his father's, three of which survive for violin as well as in more or less embellished versions for one or two harpsichords.[7] For either composer, the embellished alternate version is always highly imaginative and at least as effective as the original. But recasting a solo part in a concerto remained a relatively simple proposition, since it required little more than substituting one type of solo passagework for another, usually in the form of idiomatic types of *Brechung*. The only structurally important material of the work, the *ritornello* theme, might receive differing types of ornament when taken up in one of the solo sections, but it usually retained its original form in the tutti statements. The varied versions of H. 150, however, seem to imply that Emanuel's thematic material is also inessential and open to variation, even at crucial points in the structure, provided that it preserves the same rhythmic outline as the original.

Such thoroughgoing variation would probably be impossible—certainly it would require more ingenuity—with the thematic material of a fugue by Sebastian Bach or a sonata by Haydn. The former would require maintaining the special polyphonic capabilities of the original, such as the potential for *stretto* or inversion, while in the latter the very continuity of a developmental section might depend on the successive transformations of a simple motive, which would have to retain its identity in the varied version.

But the figures (*Setzmanieren*) with which Bach constructs his material are not subjected to either the contrapuntal techniques of Sebastian Bach or, in most cases, the intensive development which Haydn characteristically applies to important motives. Emanuel does "develop" motives by using them in sequences or by altering the harmonic plan of passages which recur in different sections of a work. Yet in neither case is the motive itself articulated in such a way that it or its development is an essential part of the process. Another motive might as well have been used. This is illustrated by variant readings between the autograph and the first printed edition of the piano trio H. 525 (*W. 90/3*). The first divergence between the two versions is in measure 9, where the print substitutes a more drawn-out arpeggio for the simple triplet of the original:

Ex. 4-15.   Piano trio in C (1775), H. 526 *(W. 90/3)* 1/8-10, a)
             from autograph (P 358), and b) from
             print (Leipzig, 1776). Strings omitted.

When the second section of the movement reaches a parallel passage, the autograph retains the original triplet motive, but the print varies it for a second time, retaining the original bass. (Ex. 4-16) Presumably Bach altered the passage before publishing it in order to avoid the disturbing interruption of surface motion occasioned by the rests of the autograph version in measures 9 and 10. This is Oberdorffer's reasoning, at any rate, who gives the printed version at this point in an edition otherwise based on the autograph.[8] But the melodic and rhythmic surface of these measures—their motivic content, in other words—is largely incidental to the harmonic progression and the structural function of the passage, which is to commence the modulating portion of each section. Thus the printed version can alter the original melodic idea, and even vary it further at measure 50, without any significant effect on the piece as a whole. The result is a work which requires the use of discrete motives (*Setzmanieren*) to articulate the harmonic rhythm, yet in which little

Ex. 4-16.　　Same, mm. 50-51, from a) autograph, b) print.

depends on exactly what shape the motives take, or on when and how a particular motive is reused in the course of the piece.

The inessentiality of Bach's motivic work is particularly clear in a number of keyboard movements composed almost entirely out of arpeggiation. Published examples include the opening movements of the Sonatas H. 5 (*W. 65/3*) and H. 244 (*W. 55/1*) and the Andante of H. 42 (W. *65/14*). These are among the movements which Berg describes as being "in perpetual motion," comparing them with certain preludes of Sebastian Bach.[9] But Emanuel Bach's movements of this type are distinct from both the arpeggiando prelude of the Baroque (examples of which occur among Emanuel's keyboard fantasias and *solfeggi*) and the Classical *moto perpetuo*. Despite the homogeneity of the material, these movements are organized in precisely the same formal patterns as Bach's other sonata movements, although the absence of strong contrast in texture or material leaves this sort of movement colorless in relation to some of Bach's other works. While the constant arpeggiation, unlike that of a Baroque prelude, undergoes constant modification through irregular *acciaccature*, changes of pattern, and so forth, the variations of detail are of little importance beyond the surface.

Emanuel's attachment to sonata form irrespective of the nature of his motivic material becomes evident when one considers that he could write two sonata movements that are formally analogous in every way while creating the surface through fundamentally unlike methods: unbroken arpeggiation, as in the "perpetual motion" movements, and strict invertible counterpoint, as in the last movement of the sixth Württemberg sonata. Whereas the elder Bach confines each technique to its proper genre—the prelude and the two-part invention, respectively—the son incorporates both into binary or ternary sonata form, without making any adjustment in the fixed scheme of the latter. There is one important work in which Sebastian does something similar: the Goldberg Variations, which are in effect a set of one-movement "sonatas" in different genres all composing-out the same harmonic-contrapuntal *Satz*. Emanuel composes his sonatas through the same principle, but the larger proportions of his design and the greater diversity of material in each movement frequently lead to a tension between form and content which is absent in the Goldberg Variations. Hence the manneristic effect noted by Rosen: "Carl Philipp Emanuel Bach's most striking passages . . . exist in and for themselves, with little relation to any conception of the whole work."[10] This is certainly true insofar as it refers to striking *Veränderungen*: gestures, such as the triplet figure in Example 15a, which break the continuity of the surface but are still essentially ornamental in nature. Yet Bach's surface is not an entirely uncontrolled proliferation of ornamental ideas; a sense of motivic consistency or economy may prevail, most obviously in those movements based on continuous arpeggiation.

Other types of motive may be singled out for intensive use. In the slow movement of the great concerto in D minor, H. 427 (*W. 23*), the texture is permeated at various levels by an appoggiatura or "sigh" motive. The movement as it is now known is a rather heavily embellished revision of an earlier version, the opening of which can be reconstructed from the surviving fragment.[11] (Ex. 4-17) The appoggiatura idea, clear enough in the earlier version, is later embellished to the extent that it is difficult to speak of the underlying idea—half-step motion in the outer voices—as a theme or motive in the usual sense. Schenker and some of his followers would regard it as such,[12] but it seems better to understand such a "motive" as it really is: a progression or *Satz* from which the theme of the final version is derived. Still, Schenker probably would have been pleased to note that the underlying harmonic-contrapuntal idea, clear enough in the original version, was the primary inspiration of the movement, not only in the striking opening measures but in several later passages. (Ex. 4-18) In both cases the final version further embellishes the original appoggiatura, pushing it deeper beneath the surface but never quite obscuring the relationship with the opening idea of the movement.

Bach's compositional process in the last few examples clearly involved the progressively more florid "variation" of the original idea. Such treatment of a motive is quite distinct from development in the Classical sense. Similarly, when Bach repeats a motive in a new harmonic context, as in his use of the triplet motive in Example 4-15a, the effect is not so much a development as an incidental use of the motive to compose out a new harmonic progression. The

Ex. 4-17.   Concerto in D minor (1748), H. 427 *(W. 23)* 2/1-2, a)
             final version, b) reconstruction of earlier version, both
             from autograph (P 354).

fact that the new progression falls within a passage formally analogous to the earlier one only emphasizes the difference from true Classical development; in a mature Classical development selected motives return with pacing and phrasing which are usually quite unlike those of the exposition. There is no such re-interpretation in the middle section of Bach's ternary form; hence the ease with which the printed version of the piano trio (in Example 16b) substitutes a new "variation" of the passage.

That Bach is capable, on occasion, of real motivic work is proved by some of the concertos in their relatively intensive use of one or two ideas from the opening ritornello. This might be an outgrowth of the practice of using motives from the ritornello to accompany or punctuate the solo sections, as in the last example. The first movement of the Concerto H. 441 (*W. 31*) goes somewhat farther in developing two ideas juxtaposed in the opening measures—a turn and a broken chord.[13] (Ex. 4-19) The two ideas occur with particular urgency at crucial moments in the three main solo sections, first near the end of the initial solo. (Ex. 4-20) Here the violin/bass opposition of the opening measures is transformed into a solo/tutti alternation (mm. 89-92), then accelerated in an exchange which reduces the two ideas to their essential motivic content (mm. 93-4). Further motivic development occurs—to highly dramatic effect—in the second solo section.

Ex. 4-18.   a)   Same, mm. 87-90, final and earlier versions.

motivic development occurs—to highly dramatic effect—in the second solo section.

In light of such examples it does not seem quite fair to say, as Tovey did, that "C.P.E. Bach never shows an inkling of the special idea of 'development' in sonata style."[14] A work like the C-minor Concerto (H. 441) does indeed employ the techniques of Classical development, though real motivic work stands side by side with less rigorous procedures. But because there is no single central development section, even H. 441 reveals a more or less even distribution of developmental passages between the four solo sections. No one section is distinguished by a fundamentally different type of development of the material,

b)   Mm. 94-95.

Ex. 4-19.   Concerto in C minor (1753), H. 441 *(W. 31)* 1/1-3,
viola omitted.

although a substantial portion of the second section is given over to solo
passage-work. Such passage-work, however, is far less dramatic than the
passages involving real motivic development, which helps explain why, in
many concerto movements, the restatement of the virtuoso figuration in the
final solo section represents a lessening of tension, not an anti-climactic
repetition of the dramatic centerpiece of the movement. To be sure, usually
there is no such centerpiece, only occasional moments of heightened drama

Ex. 4-20.   Same, mm. 89-96.

within the context of a given solo section. The recapitulation of material from the middle section is precisely equivalent to the recapitulation of material from the first section; because the general degree of tension remains constant through all three principal sections, Bach is free to flesh out the final section with material taken from any or all of the preceding parts of the piece.

A few sonata movements, notably the keyboard Sonata H. 21 (*W. 65/11*)1 and the flute Sonata H. 555 (*W. 128*)2, follow the concerto pattern of introducing passage-work in the second section. But this would seem to be only a particularly virtuosic way for a sonata movement to express a principle shared by all of Bach's sectional forms—that the material occurring between the opening and closing phrases of each section is less highly controlled, more open to variation or reordering, than the opening and closing passages. Indeed, the basic binary and ternary forms could be viewed as frameworks for improvisation, free successions of ideas and modulations set between more clearly articulated opening and closing themes. Within the central portion of each section there may be a certain consistency of material, but this fact has little consequence for the structure of the movement as a whole.

From a Classical point of view works such as the revised version of the piano trio may seem loosely constructed, since new "variations" are substituted arbitrarily for the original motive in parallel passages. All three sections of one sonata movement may employ the same motives in the same order; another movement wlth identical tonal design and phrasing may introduce new ideas in the second or third section, leaving material from the first section unrecapitulated.[15] The proliferation of material and the emphasis on variation over motivic development are sources of the incoherence which some writers find in Bach's music; given such a situation it is hard to find a strong relationship between material and structure. Yet some modern commentators have been too quick to seek in Bach's music the type of motivic work and thematic contrasts more typical of later, more Classical, styles. Such a view focuses too closely on the melodic material and its potential role in articulating a dramatic tonal design. With Bach that potential is usually unrealized—which is only to say that he is not a Classical composer. As with many of his contemporaries, the material is essentially an emmanation of the bass line and its harmonic "realization," far less significant in its own right, either as melody or in its motivic working-out, than most Classical material. Despite embellishment and fragmentation in the melodic surface, the underlying voice-leading remains generally smooth while the harmonic rhythm stays fairly constant throughout a given movement. This insures coherence at the local level even if the material seems quite arbitrary at times. Bach's rhythm and phrasing sometimes seem as arbitrary as the material, yet these too can often be understood as "variations" on a few basic schemes in much the same manner as the melodic material.

5

Rhythm, Phrasing, and Articulation

Rhythm

Most of Emanuel Bach's works have a consistency of motion similar to that of
Baroque music. This is especially clear not only in the occasional keyboard
movements which adopt a thorough-going arpeggiation, but in the many pieces
built upon Baroque dance rhythms. Berg noted a few movements from sonatas
which name dances in their titles or tempo indications,[1] but beside these there
are many more movements which adopt the regular metrical patterns of certain
dances without being labeled as such. Gigue rhythms occur frequently in final
movements, as they do throughout the eighteenth century; sarabande rhythms
are common in the slow movements. Among other survivals of Baroque
rhythm, Berg mentions the "walking continuo-style basses, and fast harmonic
rhythm" prevalent in the early keyboard sonatas.[2]

One of the first and most important twentieth-century students of
Emanuel Bach, Rudolf Steglich, drew a contrast between the first movement of
the trio-sonata H. 567 (*W. 143*), written in 1731 under the direct or indirect
influence of Corelli, and the slow movement of the sonata H. 282 (*W. 59/3*) of
1784. Steglich described a change from the "uniform pace" (*gleichformigen
Tritt*) of the earlier work to the "loosening of the rhythmic element"
(*Lockerung des Rhythmischen*) in the latter.[3] Yet a comparison of the two
works shows that the change involves only the melodic surface. The walking
bass and regular harmonic rhythm of the trio movement are clear from the
outset, and the pattern changes only slightly with the onset of passage-work (m.
53) or with the statement of the theme in the bass (m. 5):

Ex. 5-1.   Trio-sonata in B minor for flute, violin and continuo
(1731, revised 1747), H. 567 *(W. 143).*

a)   1/1-7.

b) 1/53-56.

In the keyboard movement there is greater variety of melodic figuration, but
the movement nonetheless adheres quite closely to a regular harmonic
rhythm—derived from the sarabande—in the opening theme and its varied
returns:

Ex. 5-2.　　Sonata in B-flat (1784), H. 282 *(W. 59/3).*
　　　　　　a)　2/1-2.

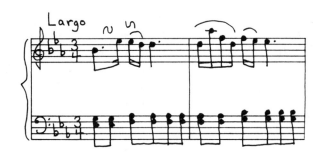

　　　　　　b)　2/16-17.

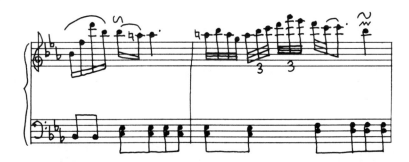

A few less pervasive rhythmic traits are also ascribable to lingering Baroque habits. Berg notes a tendency for ideas initially stated in one half of the measure to recur in the other, especially in early works in common time:[4]

Ex. 5-3.　　Sonata in G (1736, revised 1743), H. 15 *(W. 65/6).*
　　　　　　a)　2/1-2.

b)   2/11-12.

This is closely related to the practice of inserting a single measure of 2/4-time into a movement in 4/4. Bach avails himself of this stopgap with surprising frequency, not only at double-bars, as in several of the Prussian and Württemberg sonatas, but occasionally within the course of a single section.[5]

Ex. 5-4.   Sonata in G for harp and continuo (1762), H. 563 *(W. 139)* 2/73-76.

Such practices are a sign that the rhythm of such pieces retains the homogeneity or interchangeability of beats which, as Rosen notes, characterizes some Baroque rhythm.[6] Thus, in the type of movement illustrated above, every odd-numbered beat is strongly marked, with little differentiation between beats one and three. With Emanuel Bach the metrical homogeneity of such movements may be combined with a certain diffusion of the pulse, as the latter becomes heavily sub-divided through complex melodic figuration. This is especially characteristic of the leisurely sort of movement met in the opening Allegretto of the Trio-Sonata, H. 570 *(W. 146)*:

Ex. 5-5.   Trio-sonata in A for flute, violin and continuo (1731, revised 1747), H. 570 *(W. 146)* 1/1-3.

But despite the typically *galant* alternation of triplets and ordinary sixteenths, the example is still quite close in texture to the more consciously "Baroque" writing in Example 5-1. Both rely on a succession of two-beat melodic fragments set over a walking bass in eighth-notes. Though the melodic writing in Example 5 shows greater variety, rhythmically and motivically, the meter remains essentially duple, as in Example 1. Yet by comparison with Example 1, Example 5 requires a slower pulse—borne out by the respective tempo markings—and the result is a weakening of the forward impulse of the walking continuo line.

The elegant (or fussy) melodic line of Example maintains a *galant* smoothness despite its fragmentation into many small one- and two-beat melodic cells. But in other works a less regular subdivision of the beat may include unexpected syncopations, "convulsive accelerations," and other variations in surface activity,[7] as well as various types of weak phrase endings. Thus a steady underlying motion, usually maintained by the bass, coexists with a highly variegated rhythmic surface in the treble. The latter weakens the sense of ongoing impulsion, diffusing what Berg calls the "energy typical of the baroque."[8] Such rhythmic diffusion is not understood here as a stylistic problem; on the contrary, the subdivision of the beat and the consequent softening of the Baroque motoric impulse are essential elements of Bach's style. Metrically weak figures, especially the long appoggiatura and its resolution, play an important role in the diffusion of the motor rhythm. Naturally, the term "weak" is employed without a pejorative sense; a weak ending is understood simply as an embellishment of the basic impulse. The comprehensibility of such embellishment, as well as of Bach's more radical rhythmic surprises, rests on the establishment of a basically homogeneous continuity, as in the conventional sarabande rhythms or walking basses of the previous examples.

Rosen speaks of a "sequential continuity" in Baroque music, sequence being, in his view, "the most basic development of High Baroque rhythm."[9] The Classical corellary to the Baroque sequence is the periodic phrase, which, though by no means always a simplistic structure of four-plus-four measures or the like, is based on the principle of balanced, more or less symmetrical statements of antecedent and consequent. Though Bach uses such structures in his less sophisticated pieces, such as the simple rondo movements found in the second or third place of some of his sonatas, he made little attempt to put such phrasing to use in the more ambitious genres. He never learned, as Haydn and Mozart did, how to manipulate such phrasing toward serious ends, and to the end of his career his phraseology is essentially that of the Baroque; each section of a movement in a concerto, symphony, or serious keyboard sonata normally begins with a single expository phrase, extended by sequence.

Such sequences occur at two levels. At one level is the traditional type of sequence inherited from the Baroque: three or more statements of an idea at different pitch levels, a composing-out of a diatonic line in the middle-ground. On a larger level occurs what will be called a sequential repetition—the repetition of (usually) an entire phrase in a new key. This type of sequence bears a superficial resemblance to the Classical period, since both consist of two symmetrical phrases. Yet the very exactitude with which the second phrase of a sequential repetition repeats the first gives it a formality, even a stiffness, which is quite opposed to the flexibility of the Classical procedure. While the smaller sort of sequence may or may not involve a real modulation, the sequential repetition always does; it usually occurs at the head of the second section, just after the double-bar in a sonata form. In either case the sequence is less an expression of Classical symmetry than an indication of Bach's tendency to conceive the surface of the music as the "variation" of a relatively conventional underlying progression. Schmid noted the "preference of the Berlin school for repetition (*Tautologie*) and sequence in melody," tracing the use of sequence in the woodwind sonatas to passages in the trio-sonatas which involve imitation between the upper parts,[10] as in the "canonic" sequence illustrated in Example 4-1. But not all sequences involve such pseudo-polyphony, and the prevalence of "canonic" sequences in the trios seems more effect than cause, only one further manifestation of an underlying sequential continuity.

As noted in Chapter 4, sequences arise out of the diatonic voice-leading so common in Bach's music. Because the diatonic bass (as well as the other lines) tends to move at a regular rate from one essential tone to the next—i.e., establishes a regular harmonic rhythm—sequence results whenever successive bass tones are prolongated or "varied" by similar material. Even opening ideas

are often sequential, as in Example 4-2, and until the fifties it is a rare opening
theme which is not quickly followed by sequential *Fortspinnung*. But Bach
differs from his Baroque predecessors in frequently embellishing the material
of a sequence or varying its dynamic in successive statements of the sequential
pattern. Thus a passage from the Sonata H. 32 (*W. 49/4*) uses three different
imitative figures to work out the descending steps of a diatonic sequence:

Ex. 5-6.   Sonata in B-flat (1742), H. 32 *(W. 49/4)* 2/20-24.

Here the imitation of the last of the sixteenth-note figures by the bass stretches
the last harmony of the sequence out over a full measure, extending the
four-measure sequence into a five-measure phrase that elides into the following
one. The extension stems from the ambiguity, introduced in the second
measure of the example, in the antiphonal relationship between the parts in this
"canonic" sequence. While in the first measure the inner voice leads in stating
the sixteenth-note idea, it is the upper voice which first *varies* the idea in the
second measure. By the third measure of the sequence the upper voice has
become the leading part, imitated by the bass as it approaches the cadence to D.

The melodic embellishment and subsequent rhythmic ambiguity of the
passage hardly mask Bach's routine reliance on sequence in this and in similar
bridges. The sequences become objectionable when they fall into prosaic

regularity: any proponent of Bach's music can only be embarrassed by such passages as the following.

Ex. 5-7.   Sonata in F (1740), H. 24 *(W. 48/1)* 3/41-56.

Such a passage is perhaps excusable in one of Bach's Prussian sonatas, in which his style is still a bit tentative, but an equally embarrassing sequence turns up, oddly enough, in the exactly analogous spot in the first Württemberg sonata, H. 30 (W. *49/1*). In such cases one might well complain with Berg of the "overlong and mechanical effect" of the sequence, [11] which serves as an uncharacteristically unimaginative way of extending the conventional thematic statement at the head of the second section.

The retransition is another type of bridge passage in which Bach routinely employs sequence, usually as a brief, rhythmically weak phrase set between two strong articulations, the second cadence and the return (mm. 73 and 82, respectively, in the following example). (Ex. 5-8) Here the weakness of the retransition is emphasized by its *piano* dynamic, which gives it the quality of an interpolation or insertion. This in fact is the role of the passage; it would not be inconceivable for the return to follow immediately upon the second cadence, as it does in some other sonata movements, and it is perhaps for this reason that Koch describes the retransition as an appendage to the second *Period*. [12] Because Bach's sonata form is not conceived as a continuous

Ex. 5-8.   Sonata in B-flat for flute and continuo (1738), H. 552
            (W. 125) 2/72-83.

dramatic process, the tension generated in the course of the second section is largely dispelled at the cadence, prior to the return. Thus the retransition need not be anything more than a short unobtrusive connecting passage—a role for which a simple descending sequence, as in Example 8, is well-suited.

Several exceptional retransition passages occur in the Württemberg sonatas (W. 49); one in the Sonata in A minor is as lengthy (in proportion to the rest of the movement) as the retransition solos in certain concertos. Here the retransition is expanded using an arpeggio motif derived from the closing theme.

Ex. 5-9.   Sonata in A minor (1742), H. 30 *(W. 49/1)* 3/104-29.

The passage is a rare instance of Bach's creating a significant tension within the retransition. Like so many other retransition passages, however, this one remains sequential, its character altered through the prolongation of each harmony over a longer period and with more active figuration than is usually the case. Perhaps the most distinctive feature of this passage is not the use of virtuoso figuration derived from the closing theme, but rather the absence of a half-cadence at the end of the retransition, which makes possible an unbroken drive into the return (m. 128). This contrasts with the more typical case of Example 8 where the retransition is, in a very real sense, expendable.

The passage in the last example is one of the most dramatic in all of Bach's sonatas, which tend to be more lyrical than dramatic. Similar dramatic gestures in other works function in much the same way; they stand out as momentary departures from the pacing or harmonic rhythm that reigns elsewhere in the work. Even where Bach opens with such a gesture, he quickly falls back into his usual "sequential" continuity. The Symphony H. 655 (*W. 180*) opens with a flamboyant arpeggio in the violins—a sort of inverted *coup d'archet*—and for the first six measures simply prolongs the tonic harmony. But beginning in m. 7

Ex. 5-10   Symphony in G (1758), H. 655 *(W. 180)* 1/1-13, from
the keyboard reduction, H. 191 (*W. 112/13*, also listed
as *W. 122/4*).

Ex. 5-10. (continued)

the bass, which has been oscillating between g and f♯, begins to move sequentially down the scale in half-notes, establishing a harmonic rhythm which is maintained even when the sixteenth-note pulsation comes to a halt in m. 12. The remainder of the movement stays locked into this sequential harmonic rhythm despite a few additional interruptions of the surface motion.

Raised to a higher level, sequential motion becomes movement by sequential repetition. Such passages are especially common at the head of the second section of a binary or ternary movement, where they usually rework the main theme. Typically the first statement of the theme is in the dominant, the second in the tonic, resulting in the so-called premature reprise.[13] This procedure is routinely used from the beginning of Bach's career, as in this early sonata movement:

Ex. 5-11   Sonata in F (1731, revised 1744), H. 3 *(W. 65/1)* 3/51- 66.

Ex. 5-11. (continued)

The premature reprise serves as a passing tonal area touched upon on the way to the subdominant. While this gesture *through* the tonic is perhaps the most common sort of sequential repetition in the earlier sonatas, by the mid-forties the second statement is frequently in some other key, such as vi. Quite clearly, then, the premature reprise is merely a special case of a common modulating procedure.

The sequential repetition at the head of the second section represents a sort of structural elision: it is a way of commencing the modulating *Fortspinnung* of the second section without first stating the theme in its original form and bringing it to a cadence. Instead, the theme itself is converted into a unit of a sequence. The third section of a ternary form can likewise open with a sequential repetition. But occasionally Bach uses the sequential repetition in such a way that the return to the tonic occurs as the *second* part of the sequence. This occurs as early as the sixth Prussian sonata:

Ex. 5-12.   Sonata in A (1742), H. 29 *(W. 48/6)* 1/81-98.

Ex. 5-12. (continued)

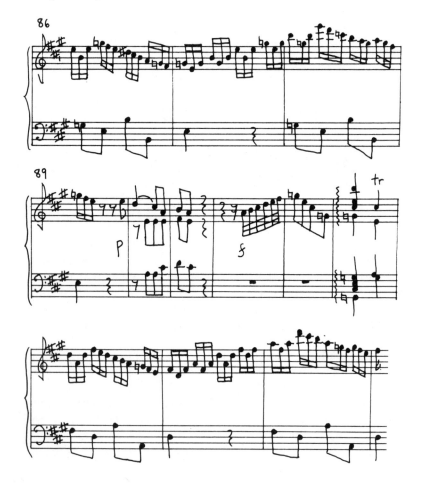

Here the first statement of the theme is in the supertonic, prolonging the closing harmony of the second section.[14] Not only does the return (measure 90) occur in the middle of a sequential repetition, but it is neatly embedded between an arrival on the *minor* dominant (E minor, as iv/ii, in measure 89) and the traditional post-return move toward the subdominant (after bar 95). An astonishing development of this technique occurs in the second movement of the Symphony H. 657 (*W 182/1*), in which the return (in E major) follows upon an initial statement in D minor. The passage depends on the parenthetical nature of the few bars in D minor, which is tonicized only at the very end of m. 27.[15]

Ex. 5-13.   Symphony in G (1773), H. 667 *(W. 182/1)* 2/26-33.

Even the first section—hence the opening theme—may commence with a sequential repetition. This occurs chiefly in late works, especially in the final movements of several symphonies, such as H. 658 and 662 (*W. 182/2* and *182/6*). In each of these works the opening sequential repetition continues a modulation begun in the coda of the preceding movement, which leads without a break into the finale. Special care is given to the restatements of the theme later in the movement, so that in H. 662/3, for example, the first ending of the first section leads smoothly back to the out-of-tonic opening:

Ex. 5-14.   Symphony in E (1773), H. 662 *(W. 182/6)* 3, mm. 37-
             38 and repetition (after double-bar) of mm. 1-4. Viola
             omitted.

One important consequence of Bach's use of sequential repetition is that
a relatively large portion of the *Hauptperiod* becomes subsumed within a
clearly articulated subdivision. When the sequential unit is broadly conceived,
the phrase comprising the sequential repetition can become quite expansive in
relation to the simple periods or unperiodic *Fortspinnung* which Bach usually
employs. In some of the concertos a sequential repetition at the opening of a
solo section is expanded by tutti interpolations, as in the first movement of H.
417 (*W. 14*). (Ex. 5-15) Here the embellished solo version of the main theme
alternates with a secondary idea from the ritornello (played by the tutti),
forming a period of twenty-two measures. This passage comprises more than

Ex. 5-15.   Concerto in E (1744), H. 417 *(W. 14)* 1/137-53.

one third of the central *Hauptsolo*; it balances the nonperiodic passage-work section which follows for some twenty-five measures.

Occasionally the two units of a sequential repetition may be large enough that each might be considered an articulated subsection, i.e., more than just a single component phrase of a period. This happens in the first movement of the Double-Concerto H. 479 (*W. 47*), where the second *Hauptsolo* is built around two thirteen-measure solo passages, one for the harpsichord and one for the piano. These stand in a sequential relation to one another near the center of the section. In fact the passage forms the harmonic crux of the whole movement, since the first half of the passage moves to the relative minor of the dominant (vi/V) while the second half, a fourth higher than the first, goes to the relative minor of the tonic (vi). The use of sequence at such a high level is no doubt a reflection of the existence of two solo parts; the urge to balance the statements of the two soloists throughout the movement culminates in the unusually expansive sequential repetition in the second section, where the sequential unit contains the virtuoso passage-work normally found at this point in a concerto with one solo part.

Something similar occurs in many trio-sonatas where the opening theme is introduced in two imitative entries by the upper parts. While such imitation is probably a reminiscence of the polyphonic tradition from which Bach inherited the *genre* of the trio-sonata, Bach's typical trio theme is too long and contains too many separate melodic fragments to be regarded as a true fugue subject. Such a theme is in fact a lyrical effusion hardly distinguishable in form or style from the themes of solo works, and the successive thematic statements in I and V (or in other keys at the heads of the later sections) can be heard as forming a sequential repetition instead of fugal statement and answer. This is particularly the case when the continuation of the first voice furnishes only an insignificant accompaniment to the answering statement of the theme, as it usually does. The opening subject of the clavier-and-violin sonata H. 511 (*W. 75*) even includes a passage in parallel thirds and sixths, stated first by the right hand of the keyboard part and later "imitated" by violin and keyboard together:

Ex. 5-16.   Sonata in F for keyboard and violin (1763), H. 511
             (W. 75).
             a)   1/1-4.

Ex. 5-16a. (continued)

b)   1/9-10.

The true model for such works—and for that matter the Double-Concerto—may well be the operatic duet, which had similarly lost most of its Baroque contrapuntal character by Emanuel's day. Beside lacking any real polyphony, the opening of such a work shows a more important divergence from the fugal design of, say, Sebastian's trio-sonatas, in the character of the modulations taking place in the opening thematic statements. The trio-sonata for two flutes and continuo, H. 580 (*W. 162*),[16] opens with a theme of sixteen measures which is imitated exactly at the dominant. Since the theme includes the modulation from I to V, the result upon imitation is a sequential period ending on V/V. This serves to confirm the original modulation to the dominant—something which rarely occurs in fugues, in which lasting modulations are reserved for the episode following the completion of the exposition.

A final illustration of sequential continuity at the large level deserves mention. The best-known example is at the opening of the Symphony in D, H.

663 (W. 183/1), which opens with successive statements of the main idea on I, vi and IV. An earlier instance of the same device occurs in each of the three sections of the last movement of the F-minor sonata H. 40 (*W. 62/6*). The first two appearances of the idea are illustrated. Though the harmonic progression and the disposition of the material are varied each time, the basic idea—motion in one part against a dominant pedal in the other—remains constant. The

Ex. 5-17.   Sonata in F minor (1749), H. 58 *(W. 62/6)*.
        a)   3/13-24.

        b)   3/75-86.

linear character of the sequence is quite explicit in the movement from one pedal note to the next. But there is also a slight sense of empty rhetoric (in the modern pejorative sense) in the way each section of the movement begins its bridge passage with this device. The variations in voice-leading and harmonic goal do not make the longer statements of the idea in the later sections much more interesting than when it is first heard, and ultimately the filling-out of the pattern becomes tedious. Even in the much later Symphony H. 663 (*W. 183/1*) there is a sense of redundancy as the sequential theme—initially quite striking—returns unchanged at the head of each section.

Phrasing

"Rhetorical" excesses of the type seen in Example 17 are an occasional by-product of Bach's sectional form, which tends to emphasize symmetry and parallel structure, rather than variety of function and form, between the sections. Within a given section Bach's concern is with a subtly embellished melodic line carrying an equally subtle and expressive sort of rhythmic detail. Successive sections merely vary the pattern set by the first section (with the exception of certain movements, especially the quick outer movements of concertos, which add virtuoso passage-work in the second or third *Hauptsolo*). Most contrasts are of local significance, and where sharp contrasts in texture or material do occur—as in the sharp break in the surface motion of Example 5-10 at measure 12—the contrast itself becomes incorporated into the over-all character of the work, which remains homogeneous. The clearest sign of this homogeneity is the routine reliance on sequential continuities in all sections and at a variety of structural levels.

Thus the variety of rhythm and articulation typical of a single movement of Haydn or Mozart, or even of Christian Bach, is never found in Emanuel's music. Bach rarely uses a fully articulated cadence at mid-section to distinguish the first and second key areas, and when this does occur in the first section it is not likely to occur at a corresponding point in the last. But the variety, or rather, the structurally significant contrasts of Classical form are unnecessary in Bach's music. Except in a number of relatively prolix movements in concertos and trio-sonatas from the forties and fifties, Bach's instrumental music is written on a small scale. The three sub-divisions of a typical *Hauptperiod*—opening theme, modulating *Fortspinnung*, and closing idea— each retain the character of a single phrase, even if a relatively extended one, as in the case of *Fortspinnung* expanded by virtuoso passage-work. Thus when Bach introduces some contrasting rhythm or texture, it usually occurs within an individual phrase, without articulating something at a higher, more architectural level. The result, especially in the keyboard music, is an extraordinary sophistication in the handling of phrasing and local rhythmic gestures. Bach's techniques affect the continuity and pacing of the melodic surface and the strength and position of cadences: in short, local motion, with an almost Webernesque concentration in some pieces on the motion from one starkly etched gesture to the next. Some of Bach's rhythmic devices are the source of the "caprice" or the "spontaneous and restless keyboard style" noted by various writers.[17] But although these rhythmic devices may be rooted in improvisatory fantasy and variation, the care with which "capricious" details were frequently added to works undergoing revision testifies to planning and calculation at the local level.

The simplest type of rhythmic "embellishment" is the metrical or registral displacement of foreground tones. This technique is already in use in Bach's earliest preserved piece, the little Menuet with hand-crossings, H. 1 (*W. 111*):

Ex. 5-18.   Menuet (1731), H. 1 *(W. 111)*, mm. 13-16, with figured
             bass sketch.

Here the displacements arise as part of the thoroughgoing arpeggiation, clearly inspired by such works of Sebastian's as the almost contemporary Menuet of the Fifth Partita.[18]

An extreme development of this technigue occurs in the outer movements of the Sonata H. 248 (*W. 65/47*), illustrated in Example 4-3. Berg draws attention to this sonata as one of Bach's most thoroughly "capricious" works.[19] Yet the metrical displacements and melodic fragmentation of such a work are not meant to be comical or merely jolting; they are varieties of written-out rubato employed for expressive purposes. Indeed, the second movement of the sonata includes figures which Marpurg and Löhlein call *tempo rubato* or *Rückungen.*[20] (Ex. 5-19) The syncopated repetitions in the opening measures of the example constitute what Marpurg calls *Rückung*—literally "jolting." The more common sort of syncopation in the fourth measure corresponds to Löhlein's *tempo rubato.* Both figures originate in the *style brisé* adopted by

Ex. 5-19.   Sonata in C (1775), H. 248 *(W. 65/47)* 2/3-7.

keyboard composers from the French lutenists of the seventeenth century; they are used for expressive purposes by later composers in such unlike works as the twenty-fifth variation of the Goldberg set and, adapted to the string quartet, in the last section of Beethoven's *Heiliger Dankgesang*.

In Bach's music such techniques are little more than a written-out performance practice. An effect of greater structural significance occurs when the prevailing rate of surface motion varies within a single movement. Though the homogeneous texture precludes this from happening in most of Bach's music, it can be seen in highly concentrated fashion in some of the preceding examples, such as 5-10 and 5-15 . A few works maintain contrasting rates of activity over much longer periods, creating a significant polarity of rhythmic textures within a unified meter, tempo and harmonic rhythm. David Fuller observed this in the first movement of the Sonata for keyboard and violin, H. 512 (*W. 76*), comparing it with a number of similar Berlin works.[21] A trio-sonata of this type by C.H. Graun is described in its source as a work "with two themes."[22] The thematic contrast, however, is that of ritornello to solo theme, not the dialectic of Classical sonata form in which the two themes articulate different key areas. In the Bach sonata an opening ritornello for keyboard alone, composed of idiomatic figuration, introduces a lyrical entrance by the violin, which takes the role of soloist in a concerto or aria. Despite the obvious differences in style between the keyboard and violin

Ex. 5-20.   Sonata in B minor for keyboard and violin (1763), H.
512 *(W. 76).*
a)   1/1-3.

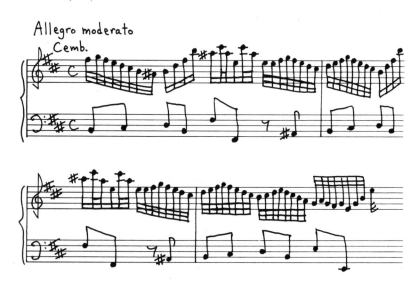

b)   1/10-12.

themes, they share the same type of bass line, harmonic rhythm, and
phraseology; both reach a cadence (or half cadence) after two measures and
continue sequentially. The contrast between them lies close to the surface, and
the two ideas can alternate in close succession without producing a break in the
continuity.

Ex. 5-21.   Same, mm. 28-30.

Eventually the keyboard figuration wins out, combining with the violin part at the end of the second section.

Ex. 5-22.   Same, mm. 62-3.

This moment, and a similar one near the very end, serve as goals toward which the movement as a whole leans forward. Indeed, the statements of the violin theme turn out to be little more than parentheses, even interruptions, within a work whose prevailing character is established by the keyboard at the outset.

Although Bach never finds a deeper structural use for such contrast within a movement, on at least one occasion the interruptions of a quick movement play an essential role in the unification of the three-movement cycle as a single entity, something which concerned Bach increasingly in later works. In the first movement of the Symphony H. 654 (*W. 179*), the phrases regularly begin with rushing string figuration only to be interrupted by one of several slower-moving ideas. The movement ends on one of the slow interruptions, which serves as a bridge to the second movement.

Ex. 5-23.   Symphony in E-flat (1757), H. 654 *(W. 179)* 1/101-2/4.

Ex. 5-23. (continued)

There is no direct thematic or motivic relationship between the slow movement and the interruptions of the first movement. Nevertheless, the process of inserting relatively static passages into the Allegro helps prepare the Larghetto, which at the largest level is itself a parenthesis between the two quick outer movements.

Perhaps the most famous application of this technique is in the *Programm-Trio*, H. 579 (*W. 161/1*). The two upper parts represent contrasting characters, one called *Sanguineus*, the other *Melancholicus*. Bach distinguishes them through different meters and material while maintaining a proportional tempo relationship between the alternating sections in which each character is presented. Thus there is, in effect, only a single basic pulse, and the harmonic rhythm in the statements of *Sanguineus* is, on the whole, exactly twice as fast as in those of *Melancholicus*.

Ex. 5-24.   Trio-sonata in C minor for two violins and continuo
(1749), H. 579 *(W. 161/1)* 1/26-36. Violin 1 represents
Sanguineus, violin 2 Melancholicus.

Ex. 5-24. (continued)

The two characters interrupt each other frequently in the earlier parts of the movements' two sections, but eventually unite in the quicker tempo, as in the somewhat later H. 512 (*W. 76*).

The many interruptions in the *Programm-Trio* involve numerous breaks in the continuity—deceptive cadences, fermatas, and so forth—all of which could probably be identified with particular rhetorical devices through the *Figurenlehre*, as Bach's preface to the work suggests.[23] Bach's description is not so much a hermeneutic program as an effort to analyze the rhythmic situation presented in the example. In fact the unexpected articulations which arise in the *Programm-Trio* through the sudden alternation of characters represent, as was noted earlier, an important aspect of Bach's rhythmic style. Even in works employing a single unified type of motion, unexpected pauses, interpolated phrases and other devices give rise to similar types of surface discontinuity. Such articulations have a more serious effect on the flow of the music than those in Example 18 and 19, where the pulse itself is unaffected by the fragmentation of the lines. The sharper breaks in continuity in Examples 23 and 24 are still, however, direct outgrowths of Bach's characteristically *galant* melodic writing through a profusion of small fragments. In these latter examples Bach takes pains to heighten the sense of fragmentation through contrasts of character, texture and tempo. Yet the fragments usually occur within a single phrase or passage of *Fortspinnung*; none is a self-sufficient phrase on its own. Thus, even the articulations in Example 24 are of only minor structural significance; the second Presto passage (measures 29-33) is essentially an interpolation into the Allegretto, and measures 26-29 and 35-36 would form a comprehensible period with or without the interruption.

Similar considerations apply to most of the empty measures and fermatas found especially in the keyboard sonatas. Even the most radical of these articulating devices tend to occur within, not between, phrases (or larger units). A. Peter Brown discusses one such passage in the second Württemberg sonata,

H. 31 (*W. 49/2*), but his interpretation places too much weight on the thematic and tonal contrast in the parenthetical passage, which is set off by a fermata on a cadence marked *adagio*.

Ex. 5-25.   Sonata in A-flat (1742), H. 31 *(W. 49/2)* 1/19-30.

The *adagio* indication is no more than the equivalent of the ritardando which a later composer would have used at this point. Brown sees here a "small dimension continuity" combined with a "larger dimension discontinuity due to a series of differing tempos;" the result is "a rhythmic energy whose drive is frustratingly interrupted."[24] While one can hardly deny the presence of interruptions in the example, it is probably wrong to hear them as "frustrating" breaks in an otherwise headlong drive to the final cadence of the section. Above both the "small dimension continuity" of the surface motion and the "larger dimension discontinuity" afforded by the *adagio* measure and other interruptions, there is a sense of coherence or unity which emerges from hearing the interrupting gestures as occurring within larger gestures. These larger gestures are no more than the customary *Fortspinnung* and opening and closing phrases of Bach's typical *Hauptperiod.*

As in other examples of Bach's sectional form, the *Hauptperiod* contains a number of interruptions of the surface motion which do not, however, articulate key areas in the Classical sense. Thus the A-flat-minor passage beginning at measure 23, which Brown views as being "in the subdominant of the dominant," is not even that; it is merely a single extended sub-dominant harmony (iv/V) and is never "in" any key other than E-flat (V). Brown seems to regard this brief touching upon the minor mode as being akin to the second theme of a sonata-allegro from—presumably because of its contrasting mode and dynamic—though he calls the passage "functionally ambiguous."[25] But the entire passage (measures 23-27) is best regarded as an interpolation within the closing phrase, which begins (already in the dominant) at measure 19. Its contrasting character is marked by its simple homophonic texture and the unusual *pianissimo* indication. But these are typical of Bach's interpolated passages (discussed below), and the unstable harmony of the gesture prevents it from functioning like a structurally significant sonata-form theme.

Passages like this one are disturbing, at least to a listener with a Classical orientation, because they exemplify what Rosen regards as a characteristic pre-Classical "lack of coordination between phrase rhythm, accent, and harmonic rhythm."[26] The strength of the articulations is not proportionate to their structural significance. Far from being a "glaring weakness," however, such ambiguity is perhaps a necessity in movements which aim at length and variety but which lack structurally functional subdivisions of the *Hauptperioden.* The sudden interruptions of surface motion, like the interpolated passages, are essentially ornamental, a means of extending a section without departing from the simple basic design.

It is instructive to compare Bach's rhythmic manner with that of Haydn, who at times seems to approach the *zergliedert* style of Bach and other Berliners. In Haydn's sonata in A-flat (Hob. XVI: 46) Rosen speaks of a series of "limping tonic cadences,"[27] fully articulated by rests (in both hands) and changes in texture. The very fullness of these articulations—and the resulting "limping" quality, which comes from the failure to establish a steady pulse or harmonic rhythm—is entirely uncharacteristic of Bach, if possibly inspired by his rhetorical manner. By the same token, the fermatas which occasionally interrupt other sonatas of Haydn have a structural significance absent in, say, the pauses of Bach's H. 31/1 (Example 5-25). The exposition of Haydn's C-minor sonata (Hob. XVI:20), first movement, comes to a pause on the secondary dominant only after a long preparation, immediately followed by the dramatic entry of the closing theme. Far from being a mere interruption, the pause on the new dominant serves to confirm, once and for all, the new key (E-flat) and to articulate the new closing idea.

The exposition of Haydn's C-minor sonata is in the three-part form described by Jens Peter Larsen, which resembles the plan of Bach's typical *Hauptperiod* in its use of two principal thematic passages enclosing a longer portion of "free *Fortspinnung*" and "series of alternating [*wechselnder*] motives."[28] But where the three parts of Haydn's exposition each include a number of distinctly articulated phrases, arranged periodically, with Bach each segment proceeds as part of a single sequential or cadential impulse, without periodic organization. Bach's chief means of expansion in each portion of the *Hauptperiod* are the repetition of the cadence and the interpolation of material within a phrase; both devices are found especially in closing passages.

In revising works Bach occasionally employs both repetition and interpolation in a literal sense, by adding new passages to existing phrases. A case in point is one of the *Kleine leichte Clavierstücke* of 1775 as reworked for keyboard duet.[29] At the point where the original reaches the double-bar, the arrangement introduces eight measures of new material before repeating the four-measure closing phrase. (Ex. 5-26) The new passage from bar 16 to bar 24 is an extension of the preceding phrase, of which the final cadence is repeated in measures 25-28. But bars 16-24 are also an interpolation, in the sense that they are a structurally inessential passage for solo instruments inserted before the restatement of the cadence by both instruments playing together.

Perhaps the first mention of interpolation in Bach's music was by Steglich, who left a rhythmic analysis of the sonata movement H. 36 (*W. 49/6*)2, using an analytic method derived from Hugo Riemann's rhythmic theory. In this view—which echoes Koch's—the passage is regarded as an elaboration of a normative four- or eight-measure statement. Steglich notes that the embedded passages (*eingeschlossenen Gruppe*) are recognizable by their contrasting dynamic or register,[30] as was the case with interpolated passages seen earlier. This is clear enough at the beginning of the movement. Ex. 5-27) But other types of interpolation, recognized through the contrasting

Ex. 5-26.   a) *Clavierstuck* (1775), H. 251 *(W. 116/25)* 13-16.
            b) *Duetto* for two keyboards (not listed in *NV*), H.
                610 *(W. 115/1)* 12-28.

Ex. 5-26.   (continued)

Ex. 5-27.   Sonata in B minor (1744), H. 36 *(W. 49/6)* 2/1-6.

character or parenthetical harmonic progression of the embedded passage, occur later in the movement. In one case the contrasting character of the interpolation could evidently be marked through a slight acceleration (*ein allmähliges Eilen*) of the dotted figures which interrupt the final statement of the theme:[31]

Ex. 5-28.   Same, mm. 42-46.

The keyboard rondos contain some extraordinary examples of interpolation; the long chromatic passage in Example 4-8a is embedded within the rondo theme. The ultimate example of interpolation is certainly the Concerto H. 474 (*W. 43/4*), which consists of a single *Allegro assai* movement into which a *Poco adagio* and a *Tempo di menuetto*—the latter in a self-contained ternary form—have been inserted after the second solo. The retransition tutti which follows picks up where the second solo left off. Later the themes of the two interpolated movements return briefly in a cadenza-like interruption of the final solo section.

Articulation and Structure

Interpolation on the scale found in the Concerto H. 474 obviously affects the structure of a work. Yet the internal structure of the Allegro movement is scarcely influenced by the fact that it is twice interrupted by contrasting movements. A few measures of transition are necessary to introduce the first appearance of the Adagio, but apart from that the inserted movements could easily be withdrawn to leave a quick movement in Bach's ordinary three-solo form. What applies to this example applies to the other instances of interpolation discussed in this chapter: apparently significant articulations turn out to have little bearing on the movement's actual structure. On the other hand, in some cases where articulations occur that might be of structural significance, Bach finds ways of obscuring or bridging over them.

In the Sinfonia H. 582—a work scored for a trio-sonata ensemble but otherwise adopting many conventions of symphonic style—Bach seems to make a reference to the strong arrival on the dominant characteristic of the emerging Classical style:

Ex. 5-29.   *Sinfonia* in A minor for two violins and continuo
(1754), H. 582 *(W. 156)* 1/17-22.

But the arrival on the downbeat of measure 18 is immediately subverted by the leap of the second violin into a chord on the third beat. This leap becomes a motive which is repeated and developed for the next ten measures or so, and the arrival itself is repeated sequentially in measure 20. Hence what at first seems like the conventional announcement of the secondary key area instead is wittily transformed into merely another motive in Bach's sequential *Fortspinnung*. The arrival at measure 18 has no particular structural significance, as the later sections of the piece demonstrate. An analogous passage fails to occur in either of the later two *Perioden*, although the unison idea of measure 17 returns to introduce the return as well as a transitional coda to the slow movement. Thus what might have been an important articulation in another style is reduced to a mere interruption of the surface here.

But even the structural articulations of Bach's form are occasionally bridged over, if rarely actually omitted. Since the obscuring of structural articulations can be taken as a manneristic device, Berg notes examples in which the second cadence is avoided in favor of a swift return to the tonic.[32] The result is at most blurring of the edge between the two later *Perioden*, for the form still depends on the preparation of a cadence toward the end of the second section. At the last minute the cadence is withdrawn through a deceptive resolution or some similar device.

A more subtle version of the same technique occurs in a number of movements which go so far as to weaken the most important articulation of Bach's ternary form, the return. This is done by making the return arise as an unbroken continuation of the preceding retransition passage, as in the third movement of the Symphony H. 664 (*W. 182/3*):

Ex. 5-30.   Symphony in E-flat (1776), H. 664 *(W. 183/2)* 3/55-60.
Winds omitted.

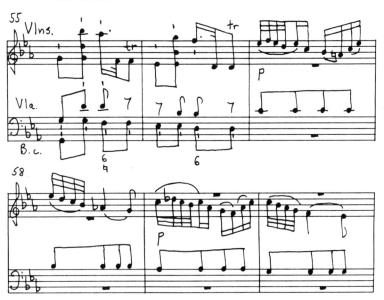

The theme, which returns at measure 57, is a sequence opening on a C-minor harmony (vi); the descending treble and bass lines of the theme form a smooth continuation of the descending lines of the preceding measures, despite the changes in texture, register, and dynamic at the return. The return itself is unmistakable, although it lacks the emphatic articulation of most of Bach's returns. The result is a witty variation of Bach's usual procedure, though one which hardly transforms the moment of return into the dramatic climax which may occur at this point in a Classical work.

Bach does, on occasion, seek to dramatize important articulations, though not in any way that resembles Classical procedure. The peculiar nature of some of Bach's transition passages, either within movements or between movements, stems from their dependence on what may be termed a suspended cadence, often followed by some sort of *non-sequitur* as in Ex. 23. The sense of suspended motion at the end of the quick movement of the symphony stems from several factors, the most important being the weak tonicization of B-flat (V) at this point; the brief reference to the sub-dominant in measures 101-102 is never quite answered, and the bass drops out on an unresolved A-natural in the lower register (bar 103). The key of the following movement does not come as a full surprise—the d″ in the first violin connects over the double-bar—but G minor is only gradually defined, the bass re-entering only with the pick-up to measure 3. G minor has not been prepared in any specific way by the preceding transition phrase, and in other works Bach uses suspended cadences as a way of making far more abrupt and unexpected key-changes.

One of Bach's favorite tricks is to end a transition between two movements with a cadence in what turns out to be the tonic of the following movement. The "tonic preparation" can be far more delicate than the familiar dominant preparation, as in the transition between the last two movements of one of the Hamburg concertos.

Ex. 5-31.   Concerto in C (1771), H. 476 *(W. 43/6),* transition
between the last two movements. Reduction of
orchestral parts as printed in the cembalo part, from
Sei concerti (Hamburg, 1772).

The Larghetto seems to come to a premature conclusion: the sequential bass, ascending by half-steps in the first four measures of the example, accelerates the harmonic rhythm in the next two without, however, making a direct root motion to C. The treble likewise avoids a conventional cadential formula, ending on the third, and the first two measures of the Allegro in fact repeat the treble voice-leading of the last bar of the Larghetto (g″ -f″-e″).

The tonic C comes as no surprise in the Allegro, since it is the key of the concerto as a whole.[33] But it is still in many respects a *non-sequitur*, made possible by the harmonic vagueness—the sense that almost any reasonably close key can follow—of the suspended cadence. This quality of the suspended cadence helps explain one of Bach's most puzzling transitions, the preparation of a return by the parallel minor of the dominant:

Ex. 5-32.   Sonata in F minor (1763), H. 173 *(W. 57/6)* 2/22-28.

Here the suspended cadence occurs at the end of a retransition which passes sequentially through the circle of fifths from D minor to C minor. The suspension of motion at bar 27 effects an elision; the sequential unit has been three measures long in passing from D minor through G minor to C minor, but the single measure of rest serves to continue the progression through the circle of fifths to F. The suspension of motion in measure 27 makes possible the extraordinary progression from C-minor to F(V♭-1). Measure 28, opening in the tonic, at first seems a *non-sequitur,* but it is clearly a continuation of the fifth-progression comprising the retransition. The return is inexplicable if taken out of context; no key is strongly prepared by the preceding measures, and other keys than F might have occurred in measure 28. But given the clear ternary form of the movement and the way in which the retransition exhausts itself, no other continuation is possible, which is to say that the return in F major seems perfectly plausible once it has occurred.

The passage in Example 32 exemplifies in a general way all of the devices discussed in this chapter. The motion that is suspended is not particularly impulsive, and the character of the articulation—the return, which after all is the most important one in the movement—is not dramatic but rather of a strangely poignant quality, a product of the unexpected breaking off of the last unit of the retransition sequence and the subsequent harmonic twist. Also contributing to the passage's atmosphere is the sense of concentration on the smallest details of rhythm and voice-leading in the florid right-hand line; for this reason the pause, though not very long by absolute standards, takes on a peculiar intensity. Such concentration is far from universal even in Bach's music; it is absent, for example, in the broadly conceived quick movements of most concertos. Yet even some opening movements in the later symphonies, concertos and piano trios attain some of the quirkiness, if not the formal compression, of much of the solo keyboard music, showing Bach's continuing preoccupation with the subtleties of articulation and phrasing.

The attention to rhythmic detail, while to a degree an essential part of all eighteenth-century music, becomes an end in itself—the chief attraction of the music—in a number of works by Bach employing what might be called the rhetorical or declamatory manner. Among these are most of the woodwind sonatas (particularly in the slow opening movements) as well as a number of early keyboard sonatas, trio-sonatas and concertos. It was in fact the "rhetoric" of Bach's style which Tovey found notable, suggesting that it was in this realm that Bach had his real impact on Haydn: "Rhetoric is what Haydn learned from C.P.E. Bach—a singularly beautiful and pure rhetoric, tender, romantic, anything but severe, yet never inflated."[34] Bach's development of a sophisticated and subtle rhetoric was a natural product of the collision between a son of J.S. Bach and the popular *galant* style.

Not all of Emanuel's adaptations of *galant* manner are successful, particularly in early works. Attempts to combine polyphony with *galant* melody and rhythm in the trio-sonatas largely fail due to the essentially monophonic rhythm. That is to say that the articulations of the three parts, or at least of the upper two, are virtually always "coordinated," LaRue's term for cases in which the parts lack any real rhythmic independence from one another.[35] Emanuel's keyboard fugues (W. 119/1-6, and a few other examples not in *WV*) suffer from similar deficiencies: an absence of deep contrapuntal interest and a tendency toward square sequences and pseudo-imitation (c.f. Example 4-1).

Some of Bach's early efforts in the rhetorical style are not entirely convincing either. The Allegro of the Sonata for oboe and continuo, H. 549 (*W. 135*), Bach's earliest instrumental sonata according to *NV*, suffers from an unrelieved series of short *zerhackte* ideas with metrically weak endings. In other works the characteristic *galant* penchant for an intricately articulated melodic line leads to some awkward divisions between phrases (or *Glieder*), as with the stuttering repeated notes at the cesuras (indicated by asterisks) in Wq.n.v.31:

Ex. 5-33.   Sonata in F (1734), Wq. n. v. 31/1/26-28. Asterisks
indicate articulations between gestures.

These are smoothened in the revised version.

Ex. 5-34.   Sonatina in F (1734, revised 1744), H. 7 *(W. 64/1)*
1/26-28.

Yet, in general, the early works, especially the flute sonatas and the W. 64 Sonatines, are remarkable for the mastery of the rhythmic style characteristic of the later Emanuel Bach. Except in detail, many movements are stylistically quite close to pieces written much later in his career. Bach's consistent care for intricate melodic and rhythmic detail thus mirrors his lifelong consistency in matters of form and compositional procedure—a few extraordinary works excepted. In many cases the form remains little more than a scaffolding for elegant—but rarely empty—rhetoric.

6

Forms

Despite Bach's increasingly sophisticated use of interpolation, echo, and related devices, the essential articulating elements of Bach's forms are limited to those found in the late Baroque dance movement and described by the eighteenth-century North German theorists—the thematic statement at the beginning, and the cadence at the end of each section. Such a form is simple, without the more numerous and more complexly related parts of the Classical sonata and its derivatives. Berg speaks of a "stiffness" resulting from Bach's habit of stating the main theme at the head of each section, and notes a tendency for tension within a ternary sonata movement to rise and fall in "three separate and more or less equivalent waves."[1] In fact the symmetry of this highly stereotyped dynamic design seems to have been exactly what Bach intended in the great majority of his sonata movements; it is, for better or worse, a defining feature of virtually all of his forms and those of his North German contemporaries.

The few exceptions among Bach's movements in sonata form prove the rule. In several early sonata movements, such as the opening movement of H. 2 (*W. 62/1*), the final section is unusually short, disproportionately so in relation to the preceding sections. Such a movement is best understood as a type of rounded binary form, distinct from true three-part form in the absence of a fully worked-out third section. In several other movements, notably the first movement of the Sonata H. 36 (*W. 49/6*), the rewriting in the final section produces a heightening of harmonic tension well above that of the first two sections, hence placing a climax of sorts in the third *Hauptperiod*. Such a movement represents a rare departure from the usual homogeneity of the three parts in Bach's ternary forms. Thus Berg is essentially right in concluding that "Bach's sonatas have a peculiar balance and logic, but for the most part, no strong focus."[2]

This last remark can be extended to the concerti, the symphonies, and even some of the keyboard fantasias and rondos. In none of these genres is there a single, central climax ("focus") in a typical movement. Despite an intense drama within the individual section, the overall conception of the form is more schematic or symmetrical than dramatic. This is true even though many pieces, notably some concerto movements and some of the rondos, have an asymmetrical form in which the later sections of the work are of increasing length. Such forms represent a peculiar development of Bach's usual formal conception, but not a fundamentally distinct type.

Modulation and Tonal Design

The essential elements in each section of Bach's sectional forms are the establishment of a tonic at the beginning, the subsequent modulation, and the drive to the cadence at the end. Regardless of the key structure, the first two cadences of a three-part form are virtually equivalent in terms of their articulatory strength and the lengths of the sections which they close off. Thus, while the first cadence is likely to be to the dominant and the second to a more distant key, the tonic/dominant polarity is not particularly strong, certainly not to the point that it over shadows all other key relationships, as in most Classical forms.[3]

While most movements are built upon a tonal scheme involving just three main areas, the relationship between these tonalities, and the means of articulating them, resemble those found in a Baroque ritornello form. In a Baroque aria or concerto movement four, five, or perhaps more "polar" keys might be established, each articulated by a statement of the ritornello theme. With Bach the number of sections (and corresponding thematic statements) may be reduced to three, or even to two, but the essential idea remains that of the Baroque form—a succession of *Perioden* each modulating to a different key and articulated at the opening by the same motive or theme. The returning idea may be varied or extended differently in each section; what is most significant is that there is almost always a *single* distinctive thematic idea heard at the beginning of each section or, in the concertos, in the ritornello. While there may also be a distinctive closing idea in each section, neither it nor any other recurring material is of formal significance. The existence of just one principal idea, together with the unitary nature of each section, distinguishes Bach's conception of form from that of the Classical style, which depends on a dialectic of thematic ideas and key-areas within each section.

Like Haydn, Emanuel tends to leave the tonic quite early in the initial *Hauptperiod*—specifically, at the beginning of the *Fortspinnung* which follows the statement of the theme and which occupies the bulk of the section. The following illustrates Bach's typical manner of passing from dominant to tonic in the opening section of a sonata movement. (Ex. 6-1) Bach's manner of establishing and then confirming the modulation to the dominant is in principle the same as that which would have been employed by any of his contemporaries. Following the statement of the theme in mm. 1-6, the work moves, chiefly by sequence, through a series of briefly tonicized keys until it arrives on V/V in measure 18. Everything before then, including the brief

Ex. 6-1.   Sonata in D (1744), H. 42 *(W. 65/14)* 1/1-29.

Ex. 6-1. (continued)

return to the tonic around bar 14, has been transition; hence one might speak
with justice of the "migrating tonality associated with the Baroque style"[4] at
least up to bar 18, and perhaps as far as measure 26, where a (deceptive)
cadence in A finally takes place. The preceding phrase (mm. 19-26),
prolonging V/V, might be compared with the second theme of a Classical
sonata-allegro, but the analogy would be imperfect; there is no strong sense of
arrival at the downbeat of measure 18, even though at this point one is
confirmed in the suspicion that one has reached the dominant of a new key.
Far from introducing a second thematic group more or less equivalent (in size
and importance) to the first, the dominant arrival prepares the closing theme.
Indeed, the dominant prolongation beginning at bar 19 is already part of the
closing gesture of the section, as it leads directly to the deceptive cadence at
bar 26, out of which emerge the four-measure closing phrase and the only full
cadence actually made to A. Thus the modulatory process begun at measure 7
is only completed with the full cadence at the end of the section. As in a
Baroque work, the harmonic tension created by the initial gesture away from
the tonic is resolved only with the concluding cadence of the section; there are
no intermediate resting points, save the dominant pedal point at measure 19,
and it is not reinforced by any significant change in texture or type of material.

Some works present exceptions to this principle. An articulated second
theme appears in many sonata movements, as in H. 150 (*W. 51/1*)1 and its
varied versions. But on closer inspection such themes usually turn out more
properly to be closing themes, analogous to the idea at measure 26 in the
previous example. This is true even in the flute sonata in G, H. 564 *(W. 133)*,
whose first movement makes a clear arrival on V/V roughly halfway through
the first section, followed by the entrance of a new theme:

Ex. 6-2.   Sonata in G for flute and continuo (1786), H. 564 *(W. 133)* 1/11-16.

Apart from its utter lack of contrast with the initial theme, several features argue against accepting the idea at measure 13 as a second theme in the Classical sense. For one, the entire "exposition" consists of only two periods joined by a four-measure bridge; it is hard to speak of true sonata-allegro form within such small spans. Moreover, this second theme certainly *is* a closing theme, in a literal sense, since by measure 15 it has commenced the drive to the cadence with a typically *galant* triplet figure. The entire passage from measure 13 to the end of the section at measure 23 constitutes a single closing gesture.

Other works that include a "second" theme in the first section frequently fail to restate it in subsequent sections. In any case, the usual dimensions of a Bach sonata form are rarely much broader than those of H. 564/1, far too small to develop real contrasting areas. A notable exception is the first movement of the Sonata H. 186 (*W. 55/4*), which is remarkably close to the Classical style in many ways. Yet each section of the movement still employs Bach's familiar three-part subdivision—a modulating phrase framed by opening and closing themes—albeit in combination with unusually broad, periodic phrasing. Perhaps the most remarkable feature of the first section of the movement is its use of the same rhythmic figure in the left hand to mark all three principal articulations: the opening, the first arrival on the dominant, and the statement of the closing theme confirming the dominant. (Ex. 6-3a, b and c) Since the same motive marks analogous points in the two subsequent sections, the sonata achieves a degree of motivic economy somewhat unusual in Bach's keyboard sonatas—especially in one of symphonic proportions, as is the case here. The

Ex. 6-3.   Sonata in A (1765), H. 186 *(W. 55/4)*.
          a)   I/1-6.

          b)   I/11-16.

c)   1 / 27-30.

movement is superficially, but only superficially, comparable to the so-called monothematic form which Haydn favored. The initial arrival on the dominant (Ex. 3b, m. 13), though marked by the principal rhythmic motive, is the beginning not of the second key area but of the modulating bridge, as the sequential repetition of the idea two measures later reveals. Needless to say, the subsequent appearance of the motive in the closing phrase (Ex. 3c, m. 27) is not the same as its use as a second subject would have been. In Haydn's monothematic forms, as in all Classical sonata forms, the second theme is more than a bridge or a closing phrase. Moreover it usually makes a significant change in the use of the recurring thematic idea, so that there remains some contrast of character with the first key area. No such change occurs in Bach's sonata, which throughout the long first movement retains the slightly breathless quality of Bach's symphonies, notwithstanding the occasional punctuations by rests (as in Ex. 3b, m. 12).

The A-major sonata does attain an unusual degree of expansiveness through its almost Classical phraseology, the product of the pedal points in its opening and closing themes (both articulated by the same motive). Hence the work's spaciousness: for once Bach has no need for the various parenthetic devices discussed in the previous chapter. Elsewhere Bach uses sequences and harmonic digressions as the chief means of extending the period of harmonic tension—the central bridge or transition—between the opening and closing articulations of each section. This resembles the task of any late Baroque composer, but Bach's generally slower harmonic rhythm and more florid melodic writing, even in quick movements, compel him to find new ways of adding substance—both formal and expressive—prior to the final resolution. Sequential *Fortspinnung* alone is not always sufficient; hence the need for rhythmic and harmonic parentheses.

Though they frequently make excursions to quite distant keys, Bach's harmonic digressions share an important characteristic with the simpler ones of the Baroque; no matter now chromatic or even enharmonic, the essential underlying bass usually moves either by fifth or by step. Thus Bach's most distant modulations are conceived in the same manner, and express the same rhetorical sort of affect, as the chromaticism of his father and earlier Baroque composers. In a few of the late keyboard pieces there are occasional isolated progressions and even large structural designs that produce the total harmonic flux—complete negation of the tonic—characteristic of some Romantic harmony. But Bach never seems to have discovered the device used so effectively to that end by nineteenth-century composers: the third-relation.

The concertos and the later symphonies are particularly rich in various sorts of parenthetical passages, many of which go far beyond the examples given in Chapter 5 in introducing chromatic dislocations, interruptions of surface motion, and so forth. The digression itself can be subject to interruption. In the first movement of the B-minor symphony, H. 661 (*W. 182/5*), Bach's most stunning essay in that genre, a lively sequence in the opening section is diverted from its clear path toward D major by a quiet digression to the Neapolitan. (Ex. 6-4) When the same quiet idea recurs in the second section, it is interrupted in turn by a *forte* interjection that wrenches the tonality from F-sharp minor, toward which the passage had been heading, to A minor, on the flat side of the tonic and preparing a subsequent thematic statement in the subdominant. (Ex. 6-5) In its final appearance in the third

Ex. 6-4.   Symphony in B minor (1773), H. 661 *(W. 182/5)* 1/9-16.
            Chords within parts simplified.

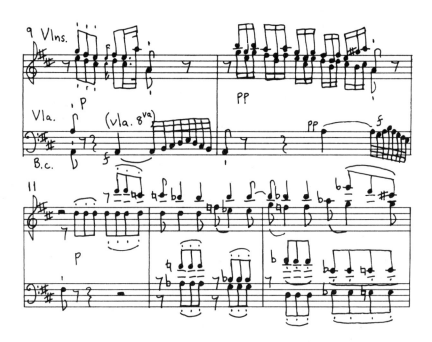

(Ex. 6-4). (continued)

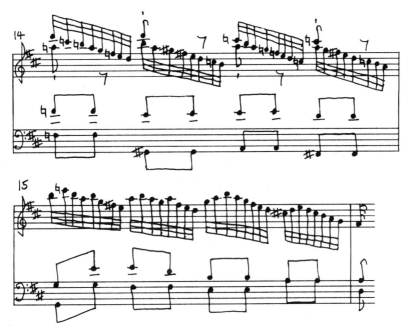

Ex. 6-5.   Same, mm. 24-31.

section the quiet syncopation of the original interpolated passage combines with the principal theme of the movement in a twelve-measure digression—a significant portion of a movement whose total length is only sixty-three measures.

In addition to its extended harmonic digressions, the first movement of the B-minor symphony is notable for an unusual, if not exactly rare, element in its tonal design; though ternary in form, it lacks a return to the opening theme in the tonic. Instead the third section begins in the subdominant and modulates to the tonic while recapitulating in order the main motivic ideas of the first section. Similar tonal designs, which resemble Schubert's recapitulations beginning in the subdominant, occur in some of Bach's trio-sonatas from the 1740's. But their use in a relatively late work is an outcome of Bach's effort after 1770 or so to enliven his basic formal scheme through unusual tonal plans. In a subsequent symphony, H.664 (*W. 183/2*), he makes an even more radical departure from eighteenth-century norms: a first movement in the major mode which makes its first, indeed its only, significant modulation—the movement is essentially in binary form—to the supertonic, via the subdominant. The movement works in part because, like virtually all of Bach's symphonic first movements, there is no central double-bar; the whole first movement rushes by as the opening part of a continuous three-movement cycle. The move toward subdominant regions is prepared quite early, by a leap to the secondary subdominant (IV/IV) in m. 11, immediately after the statement of the principal theme.

A number of Bach's slow movements—for example, that of the symphony H. 657 (*W. 182/1*)—move to the subdominant in a similar way. In such cases the result, not inappropriate for a slow movement, is the same lessening of tension which Rosen notes in similar Romantic designs.[5] But Bach's occasional flirtation with the subdominant is probably only another case of his tonal experimentation, not the product of a specific expressive aspiration. The same might be said of such devices as out-of-key openings, as in the celebrated sonatas H. 243 and 245 (*W. 55/5* and *55/3*), or openings that consist of a modulating sequence (Ex. 5-30). A particularly witty opening in the wrong key occurs in the last movement of the Concerto in G, H. 475 (*W. 43/5*): despite a preceding transition ending on a dominant preparation, the last movement begins with four measures in the subdominant. (Ex. 6-6) Later in the movement the retransition must pass from E minor, the key of the second cadence, to a return in C. Yet the central ritornello, in the dominant, opens in that key; Bach's joke applies only to the heads of the two outer sections.

Such an example suggests that Bach's harmonic surprises are used only for their immediate effect. Indeed, there are passages, especially in the late fantasias and rondos, which seem to be no more than series of unrelated shocks, with no relation to anything else in the work. Passages of comparable harmonic complexity occur less frequently in movements in sonata form. But

Ex. 6-6.   Concerto in G (1771), H. 475 *(W. 43/5)*, transition
between second and third movements. Reduction of
score as printed in the cembalo part, from *Sei concerti*
(Hamburg, 1772).

two passages from the keyboard sonatas are notable for their success in
incorporating some extraordinary modulations into Bach's rigidly schematic
form. In the first case the passage is arguably a harmonic digression: a series of
"migrating" modulations that takes place in the middle section of a ternary
form, after the key of the second cadence has already been suggested, if not
actually confirmed. In the second case, however, the second section of the
sonata movement modulates to a remote key and makes a direct enharmonic
modulation to the return.

The first example occurs in the second section of a sonata in E minor.
The principal modulation of the section is from v to iv. Mm. 24-29 state the
main theme (in v), while mm. 54-6 state the closing idea (in iv); it is the
intervening passage which is of interest. The entire passage is built over a long
descent in the bass. (Ex. 6-7) Unlike those descents seen in some earlier
examples, this one is composed-out neither through regular sequences nor
through spontaneous improvisatory gestures. Instead the bass line moves
irregularly, coming to rest in a number of pedal points that establish
momentary tonicizations, especially F minor at m. 33 and G minor at m. 43.

Ex. 6-7.   Sonata in E minor (1758), H. 129 *(W. 52/6)* 1/24-58.

Ex. 6-7. (continued)

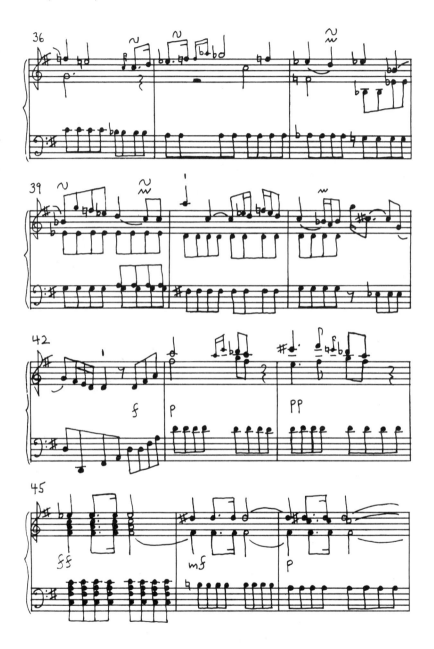

Ex. 6-7. (continued)

Ex. 6-8.   Sketch of Ex. 7 (mm. 30-57). Slurs and ties represent
            prolongations of single tones or harmonies. Dotted ties
            indicate registral connections.

These pedal points come from the opening theme; the one at m. 43 in fact bears a statement of the principal motive, but now over a dominant pedal instead of a tonic. Though brief, the tonicizations which these pedal points mark are considerably more stable than those of Bach's usual sequential *Fortspinnung*. Yet the keys they establish are not related to one another functionally; as in the A-major fantasia (Ex. 4-6) the chromatic descent in the bass supports a passage which is held together almost solely by the linear voice-leading of both the bass and the upper parts. Hence the overall harmonic instability is far *greater* than in most modulating passages, and the brief plateaus of stability reached along the way have a disembodied character; they float in some undefined tonal region apart from that of the work as a whole. While A minor seems to emerge at the end as a stable key, it is not so stable as to preclude an immediate return to the tonic, in part because the turn to A minor at m. 52 represents an unprepared departure from the preceding two or three measures, which seem headed toward E. Thus the statement of the closing phrase and cadence in A minor serve more as a digression than a fully confirmed modulation to the subdominant; they are connected to the return by the same E pedal in the bass. Indeed, this E, embellished by D and later D sharp, could be understood as connecting all the way back to m. 30 (and 27), as the dotted slurs in Ex. 8 suggest.

Even in this extraordinary series of modulations there is an early suggestion, with the diminished chord of measure 32, of an anticipation of the goal, A-minor. But the enharmonic reinterpretation of the chord (in its resolution to F minor, bar 33) and the subsequent modulations are more characteristic of the fantasias and rondos than of the sonatas. Also akin to the fantasias is the sense of structural discontinuity or interruption: measures 49-50, which correspond thematically to measures 3-4, can be heard as a continuation (in another key) of the abortive thematic statement in measures 43-44.

The suspension of functional relationships—but not of voice-leading and registral connections—seems to be the dominating tonal principle of the fantasias and rondos, where it applies over virtually the entire piece. In sonata forms, however, any suspension of ordinary tonal relationships usually occurs within the well-defined limits of one of the two or three main sections. Bach rarely violates this principle; in H. 129/1 (Example 7) the modulating passage nests cozily between the customary statements of the opening and the closing ideas. A striking exception, possibly unique in Bach's *oeuvre*, is found in the first movement of the Sonata in F-minor, H. 153 (*W. 57/6*). Though a mature three-part form, the movement lacks a true second cadence; the second section passes dramatically, without a break, into the return.

A textual problem in the crucial passage must first be resolved, since the latter has never, in several modern editions, been correctly printed. The problem involves several double-flats which are clearly indicated in the source seen here (the third collection *für Kenner und Liebhaber*, published in 1781), although the notation used to indicate the double-flat—a single flat slightly larger than usual—is easily overlooked.[6] Schenker guessed what was essentially the right reading, but relegated it to a footnote.[7]

Ex. 6-9.   Sonata in F minor (1763), H. 173 *W. 57/6)* 1/53-65.

Taking the place of a second cadence is the arrival on F-flat at measure 55. But this key is weakly tonicized if at all; there is no root motion in the bass leading up to it, and measures 54-6 represent only the prolongation of a single harmony. Indeed, from A-flat in measure 53 the bass simply descends through F-flat to C at bar 60, while the treble ascends chromatically (after measure 57) from f-flat to f-natural.

Ex. 6-10.   Sketch of Ex. 9.

The lowest staff of the example shows the bass as it would appear by notating F-flat as E-natural—in other words, understanding F-flat as leading-tone to the tonic F. While it would appear specious to regard the e-natural of the bass in measure 64 as connecting back to measure 54 or 55—the two notes are enharmonically equivalent but utterly different in function—it does not seem wrong to understand the bass F of measure 65 as filling in the register left open after measure 55. By the same token, the a-flat of the treble in measure 65 clearly answers the one in measure 54, but to draw a direct connection between them would be to raise more questions than it answers.

Schenker, in his conjectural emendation of the passage, noted the enharmonic equivalence of the chords in measures 58 and 61. Yet, despite the web of connections and the clear dominant preparation in measures 60-64, the return here is less convincing than in the preceding example. F-minor is well enough defined by the iv-I$_{6/4}$ progression in measures 59-60, but at no point is there a strong arrival on the dominant; the latter only emerges gradually in measures 60-63 after a period of tonal uncertainty. The one actual dominant harmony, in measure 62, is metrically weak, the resolution of the diminished chord in the previous measure, and thus the whole passage, from measure 57 on, leans into the return without a strongly articulated dominant. Even the bass makes only a weak neighbor motion from the leading tone into the return, so that one never actually gets a dominant chord with the root (C) in the low register. In its avoidance of an emphatic dominant preparation, the passage illustrates Bach's tendency to head straight toward a harmonic goal—in this case the return itself—without making any secondary articulations along the way. In Bach's effort to dramatize the return, he overlooks the possibility that a strong arrival on and subsequent prolongation of the dominant, prior to the return itself, might generate greater tension than a headlong fall into the tonic. On the other hand, Bach's procedure here is consistent with the small dimensions of the work, which require quick, concise tonal movement. Having worked its way to an unusually distant key, the piece has only a limited space in which to work its way back. Bach's solution is to pass directly to the tonic through the single diminished chord in measure 58. Such a harmonic *coup* is ingenious, and certainly blameless in terms of immediate voice-leading. But the whole retransition occupies a single eight-measure phrase (measures 57-64) leaning toward the return; the passage fails to focus on the striking enharmonic modulation at bar 59, which passes by without quite receiving the attention it deserves.

The passage in Example 15 demonstrates the limitations on the type of drama which can be enacted in Bach's three-part form. The passage is a brilliant but not wholly successful attempt to dramatize the return by leaving the second section open—without a closing cadence—and passing to the return in a single sweeping gesture. A dramatic return of this sort is unusual for Bach. More often the return is concealed, by eliding the retransition into the opening measures of the third section (Example 5-30), or occurs as a witty rejoinder to a thematic statement in a foreign key, as in the examples of return through sequential repetition. In neither of the latter cases is the return treated as a point of high dramatic tension. Bach's preference for an understated

Ex. 6-11.   Concerto in D (1778), H. 478 *(W. 45)* 1/47-52. Horns
omitted.

return is a product of his adherence to schematic sectional forms in which harmonic tension is generated in the course of a section and then largely dissipated in the concluding cadence. Even in concerto movements, Bach often undercuts the return—the first reappearance in the tonic of the opening material—through the device referred to here as the tutti retransition, which opens as a ritornello at the end of the second solo—hence in IV, vi, or a related key—but soon passes into a restatement of material from the latter part of the opening tutti, in the tonic. Although the subsequent solo entrance constitutes the true return, the dramatic potential of such a return is often unrealized because of the large extent of material from the ritornello which has already been presented in the original key.

The value of the tutti retransition for Bach lies not in the drama it might bring to the concerto form—it is essentially undramatic—but, as in the varieties of elided and sequential returns, in the unexpectedly smooth transition which it effects back to the tonic. A particularly elegant example of the retransition tutti occurs in the first movement of Bach's last solo concerto, H. 478 (*W. 45*). Here the solo return, at bar 52, is preceded by five measures of ritornello. (Ex. 6-11) Mm. 49-51 serve as a graceful transition from the subdominant G back to the tonic D. But these measures are taken untransposed from bars 7-9 of the opening ritornello, where they occur in a completely different harmonic context.

Ex. 6-12.   Same, mm. 5-11.

Ex. 6-12. (continued)

At measure 6, G is only a subdominant harmony, the passage in question a diatonic sequence; later G is the key of the second cadence, and the passage is used as a modulating sequence between two distinct tonal areas. A crucial change in the tonal direction of a passage is effected by minimal means, with the intent of *not* attracting attention to itself.

Variants of Sonata Form

For the most part, whatever the variations of sonata form in each genre there are no essential transformations of the basic two- or three-part model. It is striking to find a large number of pieces, even in a complicated form such as the concerto, which closely follow Koch's formal precepts. But there are occasional movements which represent more substantial departures from the basic sonata form. Some apparently irregular forms turn out only to have disguised or omitted an important event, e.g., the return, but otherwise adhere to the customary harmonic and thematic patterns. More significant questions are raised by three versions of sonata form: binary form, expecially as it occurs in several movements which combine binary and ternary characteristics; ritornello form, as found not only in concertos but in through composed movements of other *genres*; and movements from the symphonies and concertos which seem to incorporate more than the three main sections of ternary form.

Particularly in the thirties and early forties, there is a significant group of movements which, although lacking a return, nonetheless possess a second cadence and (more or less) ternary proportions. In such movements the long second "half" often leaves a sense of wandering or diffusion, especially in several trio movements which make extensive restatements of material from the latter part of the first section after reaching a distinct second cadence. Following a cadence to F-sharp minor, the first movement of a trio-sonata in A proceeds to a sequential repetition (measures 44-47) which sounds like a typical retransition:

Ex. 6-13.   Trio-sonata in A for flute, violin and continuo (1731, revised 1747), H. 570 *(W. 146)* 1/44-48.

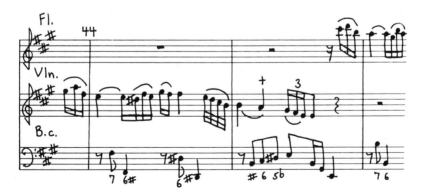

Ex. 6-13. (continued)

The material from measure 48 to the end of the movement is taken directly from the first section, thus corresponding to Koch's description of binary form. Yet the absence of a true return is strongly felt. The sequential *Fortspinnung*, which from bar 48 on is recapitulated literally from the first section, makes no special articulation at the point where this recapitulation begins; it simply extends the preceding sequential phrase without a break, confirming the tonic only by failing to modulate to any other key. The third movement of a trio-sonata in F, H. 576 (*W. 154*), is even more weakly articulated; not only is there no return, but since the second section opens with new material, the principal theme is heard only once, at the very beginning.

One early sonata is interesting because Bach's revisions of the first movement shows his increasing awareness of the necessity of adequately articulating the design. While both versions of H. 16 (*W. 65/7*)1 are in ternary form, and show chiefly figurative variants in the first section, the proportions of the later sections are altered in the revision by extensive interpolations and expansions. (Ex. 6-14a and b) In the second section the two versions run

Table 6-1. Structure of the early and revised versions
of the Sonata H. 16 (*W. 65/7*)1.

	first section (to B-flat)	second (to g)	retransition	third (to E-flat)
original version (1736)	22 measures	17	—	20
revision (1744)	24 measures	30	4	26

parallel up to bar 36 (bar 34 in the original version). At that point there is a momentary arrival on B-flat, from which the original version makes a somewhat facile modulation to G minor. The revision not only fleshes out this modulation but adds a brief retransition.

The passages added in the revision—the retransition and the expanded sequential passage after bar 36—increase the harmonic tension by elaborating the direct movement of the original toward tonal goals. The passage added at bar 37 replaces the immediate move to G minor at bar 35 of the original; later in the revised version (measures 42-45) a dominant pedal substitutes for the original V-I alternation in the bass, intensifying the structural role of the passage, which is to pause for several measures on the dominant of G minor before actually falling into the cadence. The pedal point increases the harmonic tension of the passage, and the subsequent half-cadence (bar 46) and newly inserted passage (from bar 47) further prolong the dominant and add to the sense of release when the cadence finally occurs in measure 52. Hence the G minor goal of the second section, present already in the initial version, is approached in the revision with a more developed sense of the dramatic possibilities of modulation, and the middle section grows from being the shortest to being the longest of the three periods. (The third section also is expanded in the revised version, but without significantly altering the design; instead of inserting fundamentally new passages, Bach expands the proportions through new figuration that balances the the expansion of the earlier sections of the movement.)

If Bach's revisions in H. 28/1 show a growing sophistication in the treatment of three-part form, there is no evidence of any diminishing attachment to true binary forms in which there is neither a return nor a second cadence. In these movements the passage back to the tonic is made somewhere during the *Fortspinnung* that follows the double-bar and which precedes the restatement of material from the latter part of first section. While there is, as in borderline movements like H. 570/1 (Ex. 6-13), a danger of producing diffuse or weakly directed motion in the second half, the smaller dimensions of most binary movements seem to forestall this. An outstanding example of such a movement is the last one of the F-minor Sonata H. 153 (*W. 57/6*), in which the second "half" is actually somewhat shorter than the first (thirty-four as opposed to thirty-six measures).[8] This movement serves as a relatively static, lyrical, conclusion to the two unusually dramatic movements which precede it (cf. Exx. 6-9, 5-32). The second half of the movement opens with a remarkable transformation of the opening theme that shows the poignancy Bach could achieve through the simplest means. (Ex. 6-15) The opening idea (Ex. 15a)

Ex. 6-14.   Sonata in E-flat, H. 16 *(W. 65/7).*
   a)   Original version (1763), 1/21-44. The portion in
        brackets was replaced in the revision.

b)   Revised version (1744), 1/37-58, corresponding
     with the bracketed portion of the original.

Ex. 6-15.   Sonata in F minor (1763), H. 173 *(W. 57/6)*.
  a)   3/1-4.

  b)   3/37-40.

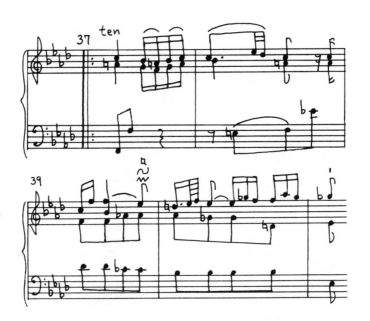

comes back in F major, by which means Bach avoids a routine sequential repetition and instead plunges immediately toward the subdominant. What would normally be a relaxation of harmonic tension—the quick move toward B-flat minor—becomes instead an intensification with the further move to a secondary subdominant, E-flat minor, by the fifth measure after the double-bar.

The transformation of the theme includes a clever reinterpretation of the cross-relation in the second measure. The bass tone E-natural, which in the original theme bears a diminished chord functioning as a dominant, becomes a chromatic appoggiatura after the double-bar. In other words, the ornamental e-flat in the second measure of the melody becomes a chord-tone after the double-bar, where the first two measures of the theme prolong a single V^7 chord in the subdominant.[9] Thus the diminished octave in measure 2 serves as more than a momentary scathing dissonance;[10] it helps prepare the turn toward distant subdominant regions in the second half of the movement, which contrasts sharply with the brightness of the relative major at the end of the first section. The movement as a whole achieves a seriousness and a consistent high level of harmonic tension rare in Bach's binary forms.

This movement is noteworthy not only for its internal form but for its position in the cycle; it is a slow final movement, and as such plays an important part in establishing the special nature of this sonata, which was recognized by at least one of Bach's contemporaries.[11] Binary form is probably more common in Bach's slow movements than in the quick outer movements of his sonatas; naturally the inner movements of most sonatas have no need even for the very understated drama of this concluding Andantino. A few relatively early slow movements, including some from the Prussian and Württemberg sets, employ a sort of rondo structure in which the theme returns several times in the tonic. In some cases, such as the slow movement of the third Württemberg sonata, H. 33 (*W. 49/3*), the returning theme undergoes a reinterpretation almost as poignant as in the last example. In fact the difference between this quasi-rondo form and a binary form with both halves starting in the tonic is slight; the "rondo" form in Bach's slow movements is an additive form, not unlike a binary form to which an extra section or two has been added. Indeed, many through-composed slow movements in binary form begin anew after the final cadence, but only in order to prepare a cadenza.

Ex. 6-16.   Sonata in B-flat (1740), H. 25 *(W. 48/2)* 2/37-42.

The cadenza, literally an elaboration of the final cadence, occurs at the fermata; similar cadenzas are called for in the slow opening movements of Bach's flute sonatas and in comparable works by other Berlin composers. The sort of cadenza played can be deduced from Quantz's dictum that it must be playable in one breath[12]; the brevity which this suggests is borne out by the many cadenzas written out by Bach himself.[13] The cadenzas in Bach's concertos, incidentally, work in a similar way; they are prepared by the solo instrument, not by a brief tutti passage, and they simply embellish the final structural cadence of the last solo section.

In many cases, particularly in later works, the slow movement becomes a mere transition passage between the quick movements. Yet some transitional slow movements retain a sort of truncated binary form, preserving the first cadence and the opening of the second half, as in the Sonata in D, H. 67 (*W. 62/13*), of which the slow movement is given here in full.

Bach's subtlety is evident in one of the details of the return (measure 7). The fourth beat of measure 1 bears a deceptive cadence (V-vi) which becomes a full cadence with the restatement of the opening idea in measure 7. The latter is then incorporated into a sequential repetition, the bass moving from G (measure 7) to A (8). Thus measures 7-8 serve to prepare the key of the next movement (D) by successively tonicizing its subdominant and its dominant, respectively.

The forms of Bach's slow movements are relatively free by comparison with the schematic quick movements, particularly in the solo sonatas. Yet even the brief transitional movement in the preceding example relies on the same essential processes as Bach's more regular sonata forms: the short thematic statement at the beginning, the somewhat longer sequential modulating passage in the middle, and the conclusion with a single cadential gesture in the new key. The impression of a relatively free form is enhanced by the absence of a double-bar after the first cadence, which in any case is to the mediant, not the dominant. Yet at least one slow movement, that of the sonata H. 18 (*W. 65/9*), was an ordinary binary form in its original (1737) version; the repetition of each half was removed when the work was revised in 1743. By the same token, the through-composed forms of Bach's concertos and symphonies, as well as a number of movements in symphonic style from the piano trios and quartets, are not far removed from ordinary sonata form. While none of Bach's eighteen symphonies has, in its final version, a first movement with an interior double-bar, the through-composed form in the opening movement of the symphony H. 650 (*W. 175*) seems to have been an afterthought; Bach struck out the repeats only after he had written two flute parts for the work. The interior double-bar remains in the keyboard reduction, H. 104 (*W. 122/2*), and in one source that contains only the original string parts.[14]

Are the through-composed quick movements of Bach's orchestral works merely ordinary sonata forms with the repeat-signs removed? Certainly this is not the case in the concertos. While the ritornello in a concerto movement is in principle a mere frame, its presence alters the way in which one hears the formally essential solo sections, which generally elide into each succeeding ritornello without the almost complete cessation of motion that occurs at the structural cadences in Bach's sonata movements. The absence of a double-bar after the first section makes possible the unusual tonal design of a movement like the opening Allegro of the D-minor concerto, H. 427 (*W. 23*), which makes its first cadence in the subdominant. Perhaps most important of all is that the proportions of a through-composed movement are less severely constrained than those of a movement in which each "half" is repeated; some of Bach's most inventive writing occurs in through-composed movements in which the later sections are, by sonata standards, disproportionately large in relation to the initial one.

What Bach presumably learned by writing concertos he applied in the first movements of his symphonies. As in the symphonies and overtures of his contemporaries, Bach opens the first movement with a fully scored theme which serves as a sort of ritornello in relation to the more lightly scored sequential material that generally follows. Such writing led Tovey to comment that Bach's symphonies are "not really on sonata lines at all" but are closer to [C.H.?] Graun's overtures or else "more or less on concerto grosso lines."[15] Indeed, the concluding thematic statement on which so many of Bach's opening symphonic movements end is functionally analogous to the concluding ritornello in a concerto, with one important additional feature— the final "ritornello" elides into the second movement. Such transitions between movements seem to have been an identifying feature of the symphony, as Bach conceived it.[16] One even occurs in the *Sinfonia* for two violins and continuo, H. 582 (*W. 156*), although there the transition passage is based on an idea from the retransition, not the main theme. A similar transition occurs at the end of the first movement of the Sonata in A, H. 186 (*W. 55/4*), a work in symphonic style despite its three-part form with repeat signs.

A more important structural feature of Bach's concerto movements or, rather, a structural problem, occurs in the portion of the movement following the second solo, which generally ends in a cadence analogous to the second cadence of a ternary sonata form. It is at that point that it becomes difficult to equate the solo sections of the concerto with the three parts of a sonata movement. Several designs are possible, depending on which of the participants in the concerto movement (solo or tutti) plays the retransition and the return. The simplest possibility is also the rarest: the retransition is omitted and the return follows in the tutti, immediately upon the conclusion of the second solo (see Ex. 6-19 below). A more common choice is the tutti retransition, a modulating extension of the third ritornello. A third way of preparing the return is in a separate solo passage flanked by two non-modulating ritornelli.

The problem is that the porportions of the various tutti and solo passages at this point are often difficult to explain, so that the third solo, while functioning as a retransition, may be nearly as long as each of the three principal solo sections. Likewise the ritornello preceding the solo retransition may be as long as the opening tutti, while the seemingly more important ritornelli at other points in the movement may be abbreviated. A particularly glaring instance of this occurs in H. 420 (*W. 17*), in which the ternary form of the movement is obscured by the presence of a retransition solo which is articulated in the same way, and elaborated to nearly the same extent, as the other sections.

Yet the essential ternary outline remains clear in all but a handful of quick concerto movements. The rare exception proves the rule. A surprisingly late

(1753) throwback to an older conception of ritornello form appears in the Allegro of H. 437 (*W. 29*).[17] Like some of the ambiguous binary/ternary sonata-forms seen earlier, this movement possesses a distinct second cadence (and corresponding third ritornello) but no return. Instead the third solo merely "migrates" from the subdominant back to the tonic, producing this very nearly symmetrical structure:

Table 6-2.   Structure of the Concerto H. 437 (*W. 29*)1. R = ritornello, S = solo. (Parallel passages are indicated by the horizontal lines joining different sections.)

Section:	1st R	1st S	2d R	2d S	3d R	3d S	4th R
Key:	A	A-E	E	E-D	D	D-A	A
Number of measures:	23	20+18	16	40	10	27+18	23

Especially unusual here is the repetition of the complete ritornello at the end of the movement, presumably to make up for the absence of any earlier restatement of the opening idea in the tonic by the tutti.

A more typical plan is that of the third movement of the Concerto H. 427 (*W. 23*):

Table 6-3.   Structure of the Concerto H. 427 (*W. 23*)1. Retr. = retransition.

Section:	1st R	1st S	2d R	2d S	3d R	Solo Retr.
Key:	d	d-F	F	F-a	a	a-d
Number of measures:	46	100	19	114	34	42

	4th R	3d S	5th R
	d	d	d
	6	82	20

The fourth ritornello, though brief, has the indispensible role of stating the return and distinguishing the final solo from the preceding solo retransition. This return is an undeniably dramatic moment, yet it is not the most dramatic point in the movement; one is most struck by the opening of the retransition solo, following a quite lengthy third tutti:

Ex. 6-18.   Concerto in D minor (1748), H. 427 *(W. 23)* 3/306-18.

The octaves at the opening of this solo suggest a new beginning—they resemble the opening of the first solo—and one consequence is that the retransition is the most strongly articulated of all the solo sections. Yet the tonality in which the retransition begins, the minor dominant, is functionally neutral, neither wholly stable nor demanding any particular resolution. Thus the opening of the retransition solo is dramatic at the local level, somewhat vague at the highest one; it is unclear how this dramatic articulation is to be heard in relation to the return, which follows quite shortly.

There can be no question, however, that the energy of the tuttis and the spirited solo sections of works like the D-minor concerto made for a dramatic intensity unprecedented in instrumental music, eliciting comments such as Koch's analogy between the concerto and classical tragedy.[18] Bach occasionally introduced concerto effects into other genres—frequently in the symphonies, as noted earlier, less often into solo and chamber works. Bach's two sonatas for viola da gamba and continuo, H. 558-9 (*W. 136-7*), introduce passages of extraordinary virtuosity in some of the *Fortspinnung* sections, as do some of the flute sonatas on a smaller scale.[19] A number of keyboard sonatas, notably the first movement of the fifth Prussian sonata, H. 34 (*W. 49/5*), emulate the solo/tutti opposition of the concerto by incorporating a thematic statement resembling a third ritornello at the end of the second section.

Although the concerto would seem to have no need for the formality of Bach's sonatas, a borrowing in that direction occurs in the Concerto in A. H. 411 (*W. 8*), whose first movement stands close to some contemporary sonata movements of Bach's by eliminating the retransition entirely.

Ex. 6-19.   Concerto in A (1741), H. 411 *(W. 8)* 1/192-95.
Reduction of score from cembalo part in *US* Wc
M1010.A2B13W8.

In fact there is a vocal model for this type of juncture: the Da Capo aria. Except for the continuous sixteenth-note motion, the cadence in m. 194 is analogous to that found at the end of the "B" section of a Da Capo form. The relationship between sonata (or concerto) form and the aria could not be more easily demonstrated: at the same time the oddly unidiomatic quality of the example shows how Bach's more usual procedure, the solo retransition, had made the concerto more genuinely dramatic than the vocal form on which it was based.

Indeed, the concertos are Bach's most overtly dramatic pieces. Yet even there the drama arises chiefly through one technique: the heightening of tension prior to the chief cadences through sequences, harmonic parenthesis, and the prolongation of the penultimate dominant harmony. While the alternation of tutti and solo may be dramatic, the presence of ritornellos, especially after the second solo, means that Bach's most succesful dramatic strokes occur within, not between, the principal sections. Bach's varying approaches to the retransition suggest his sensitivity to the problem. But at the largest level Bach's conception of concerto form remains as formalized as that of the ordinary sonata. The result, as Rosen comments, is a style which is "a little thin even at its most dramatic, and small-scale even when it achieves an effect of brilliance." Yet Rosen's corrolary, that Bach's "passion lacked wit,"[20] does not follow, unless one takes some of Bach's more extreme passages too seriously.

Bach's Hamburg works are nothing if not witty; they manage to be deeply expressive and dramatic as well, if not at the most profound level of structure. In one of the Hamburg symphonies, Bach presents his version of that quintessential Classical device, the false reprise. With Bach this takes the form of a false ritornello (since it is not in the tonic) near the end of the second section in the first movement of the symphony in B-flat.

Ex. 6-20.   Symphony in B-flat (1773), H. 658 *(W. 182/2)* 1/53-65.

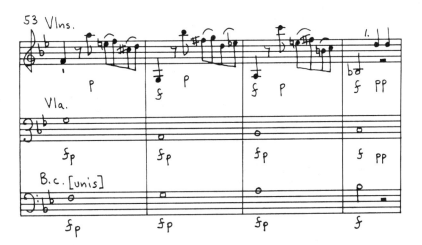

One commentator falls for Bach's deception, regarding the entrance of the principal theme at m. 61 as a third ritornello in a four-part form.[21] But the movement is in fact one of the most clearly articulated ternary movements in the symphonies, making cadences to V, iii (illustrated) and I. The brief appearance of the opening theme in E-flat at mm. 61-62 is a clever interpolation on the Neapolitan degree of D minor, blithely tossed aside by the impetuous closing theme at bar 64.

Other forms

While most movements of Bach's cyclic works employ sonata forms, a relatively small number use something else, usually a simple version of rondo or Da Capo form. Few if any of these movements are musically distinguished, despite gestures toward sonata form through the use of a retransition passage in some works. The form always retains small proportions and a simple-minded periodicity; the slow movement of the Sonata H. 118 (*W. 62/18*) is typical:[22]

Table 6-4.   Structure of the Sonata H. 118 (*W. 62/18*)2.

Section:	Theme (twice)	Modulating phrase	Theme varied	Retransition
Key:	G	G-D	D	D-G
number of measures:	4+4	4	4	4
	Theme (twice)			
	G			
	4+4			

The movement is typical in its wholly periodic construction and in the variation of one of the later statements of the theme. The same form occurs in many of Bach's keyboard *pièces*, which is not surprising in light of its similarity to the French *rondeau*.

That such movements are best described as *rondeaux* is apparent in the themes of those works which, as in H. 118/2, tend to be lyrical and discursive, not lively or "comic" as in the typical Classical rondo. Even the concluding rondos of certain piano trios, or the elaborate examples from the *Kenner und Liebhaber* sets, open with themes of the lyrical type, avoiding any suggestion of the style of a Classical *finale*. Thus Forkel, in his review of the Piano Trios of W. 90 and 91, still uses the French spelling for this "currently leading and beloved musical *genre*."[23] Forkel may not have intended to signify anything much through use of the French term; even Mozart, in, for example, the "Haffner" Serenade, K. 250, sometimes retains the French spelling, although the form and character there are far from those of the rondeaux of the French *clavecinistes*. Still, the governing aesthetic of Bach's efforts in this form is closer to that of the French harpsichord style than the more openly popular Italian. While Bach's more elaborate late rondos tend to break into soloistic figuration at some point, their initial sections fall into a form similar to that of H. 118/2.

Bach, probably suspicious of the "comic" nature of the Italian rondo, assured Forkel in a letter written in 1784 that none of his concertos up to that date had included a rondo finale.[24] But in fact by that time Bach had written a number of concerto movements which resemble rondos not only in form but in the simple periodicity of their themes. The second movement of H. 478 (*W. 45*), dating from 1778, is in fact a rondo with the first three (of five) ritornelli in the tonic. In H. 477 (*W. 44*), also from 1778, the keyboard soloist opens the third movement with a statement of the eight-measure principal theme, in clear imitation of the Viennese concert rondo. The remainder of the movement, however, is in Bach's usual three-solo concerto form, except that the first tutti ends in the dominant and the soloist, having already stated the theme at the head of the movement, avoids doing so in the following solo section. Thus while Bach seems aware of the special character of the late eighteenth-century rondo theme, he prefers to use such a theme within his customary concerto form. In the solo keyboard works actually labeled "rondo," he employs themes in his own lyrical style within a movement which owes little to either sonata form or the traditional *rondeau* and rondo forms.

The Cycle

An important aspect of Bach's form which has been largely overlooked is the care, especially in the later works, with which the (usually) three movements of a sonata, symphony or concerto are related to one another. Forkel, in his review of the Sonata in F-minor, H. 173 (*W. 57/6*), praised the work as representing a coherent program of contrasting affects in its three movements.[25] In this work the only explicit musical connection is a transition passage linking the second and third movements—actually a coda to the Andante, using material from its retransition (cf. Example 5-32). (Ex. 6-21) Because of the similar tempos, the opening of the third movement seems almost a continuation of the second, though subdued in tone by the return of the minor mode.[26] But the second movement is also linked motivically to the outer movements—to the first by the dotted arpeggios in the bass of the Andante

Ex. 6-21.   Sonata in F minor (1763), H. 173 *(W. 57/6)* 2/40-44.

theme, to the last by the *Anschlag* on the note d-flat, a motive introduced in the transition between the two movements (m. 42) and playing an important role in the Andantino.[27]

Ex. 6-22.   a)   1/1-2.

b)   2/1-2. For the opening of the last movement, see
Example 6-15a.

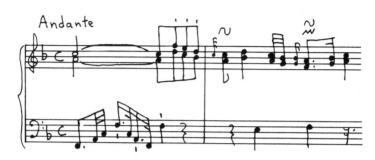

Such connections may have been one source of the unity sensed by Forkel. But there is also a profound psychological rightness in the way in which the slow final movement, with its dark second half, succeeds the Andante, whose serenity is disturbed first by its curious return and then for good by the coda. The passionate first movement, which includes one of Bach's dramatic retransitions (Ex. 6-9), ultimately finds resolution—real resolution, not the usual offsetting lightness—in the solemn conclusion of the sonata.

Few other sonatas attain the unification produced here, despite frequent connecting passages between movements. The first two movements of the Sonata in A, H. 186 (*W. 55/4*), are linked by a coda attached to the end of the first movement, in imitation of the symphonies. The first movement is in fact symphonic in its proportions and in the energy of its surface figuration (see Ex. 6-3). Yet it remains a ternary sonata form with repeat signs, lacking the concerto-like qualities that drive the first movements of most of the symphonies onward to a closing ritornello or transitional coda. Hence the appearance of a modulating coda, as a second ending bypassing the final cadence, comes as a pleasant surprise but with little motivation in what has preceded it.

At least two other works aim at cyclic unity through the reappearance of material heard earlier in the piece. In both the Sonata H. 151 (*W. 51/2*) and the Concerto H. 475 (*W. 43/5*) the slow introduction heard at the beginning of the work returns as the theme of the slow movement. This is somewhat more effective in the concerto, due to the presence of a connecting passage between the first and second movements and the addition of flutes when the theme of the introduction returns. One would like to think that these experiments reflect expressive aspirations similar to those that led Beethoven and later composers to similar devices. But with Bach these devices are essentially embellishments to the traditional forms; the cyclic procedure has no effect on the internal structures of the movements involved, and thus the idea of recalling previously heard material seems imposed onto the work, not generated from within.

Still, Bach's concern with the cycle as a whole is evident not only in the use of transition passages and occasional motivic recurrences between movements, but in the carefully calculated juxtaposition of highly contrasting movements, often depending on some dramatic effect at the outset of the following movement. A good example occurs in the D-minor Concerto, H. 427 (*W. 23*), in which the second movement opens on an unexpected dissonance (V$_{6/5/}$V; see Example 4-17). To be sure, the dramatic juxtaposition of movements, like the addition (or imposition) of transition passages or other connections, affects only the edges of the movements; the internal structures follow Bach's usual practice. Yet both procedures contribute to the impression of the two- or three-movement cycle as a continuous work. In the sonatas, because of the brevity and single-minded texture of each movement, the listener's attention shifts from the individual movement to its place in the cycle. Indeed, in some cases the sonata might be regarded as a fantasia composed of two or three brief contrasting sections—a conception not unlike that of the concluding fantasia in the *Kenner und Liebhaber* series or of the late fantasias of Friedemann Bach.[28]

As early as the 1740's, Emanuel Bach was experimenting with sonatas in which the traditional succession of movements was modified or even abandoned in favor of a continuous cycle. In one work, H. 47 (*W. 65/17*), the opening movement (in G minor) alternates between fantasia-like passages and sections reminiscent of a ritornello from a concerto or aria; this movement leads directly into a characteristically lyrical slow movement in G major. Another work, H. 60 (*W 65/24*), is in four connected movements—the only such case in Bach's *oeuvre*—and each movement ends in a key different from the one in which it begins while also avoiding sonata form. Thus none of the four movements could stand as a self-contained structure; the work is comprehensible only as a succession of movements in contrasting keys and tempos, representing a sequence of contrasting affects. That Bach was inspired, at least in part, by vocal models, is clear from the Andantino, which makes unmistakable references to recitative; the whole sonata could be viewed as an instrumental version of a late-Baroque accompanied recitative with frequent changes of affect.

By the Hamburg period Bach seems to have fully adopted the view of the whole three-movement cycle as a single ongoing process. In important late sets like W. 43 (six concerti), W. 182 (six symphonies), and W. 90 (three piano trios), nearly all the movements are linked. This principle even finds expression in the variation sets, so that Variations 3, 4 and 5 of the *Arioso* for clavier and violin, H. 535 (W. *79*), are set in contrasting keys while being linked through short transition passages.[29] Thus the individual variations, like the individual movements of the larger forms, become subservient to the work as a whole, which begins to resemble a single modulating fantasia.

One offshoot of this is that the slow movement of a sonata or symphony may be severely curtailed, as in Example 6-17. In a few sonatas the middle movement is reduced to a single bridge phrase attached to the end of the first movement, as in the Sonata H. 269 (*W. 56/4*). Other slow movements recall the fantasias in their free rhythm or distant modulation. The brief slow movement of the Piano Trio H. 552 (*W. 91/1*) contains one of Bach's most remarkable passages:

Ex. 6-23.   Piano trio in E minor (1777), H. 531 *(W. 91/1)* 2/3-6.

Harmonically conceived, it nonetheless includes a brief canon, based on the B-A-C-H motive, between the cello and the pianist's left hand. (Although the piano divides the notes of the line into repeated eighth-notes, from measure 4 the left hand imitates the cello at the fifth below.) This unusual texture—the rare independent cello part consistently forms a dissonance with the bass— makes this transition the most striking passage of the piece, despite its brevity.[30] Such transition passages remain only weakly integrated with the larger structures which they connect. While they suggest a conception of the cycle as a single unbroken process, they also suggest a fascination with the use of distant modulation or connected movements for their own sake. Often the tonal direction of the transition passage is unclear—a characteristic shared with the fantasias—and in works containing three movements, the key of the central movement may be chosen more for the perverse (or expressive) interval which it forms with the tonic of the outer movements than according to any compelling logic based on the functional relationships of the keys of the movements.

Such considerations may lie at the root of Tovey's criticism of the linkage between the first two movements of the Symphony, H. 663 *(W. 183/1)*, which he dislikes because it is in some sense an explanation of the "paradox" of a slow movement in E-flat set between outer movements in D.[31] Of course, such transitions are common in Bach's symphonies, even essential where, as in this case, the first movement reaches no full cadence. Tovey would prefer to let the unusual key of the second movement stand in clear profile, "unexplained" except by its Neapolitan relationship to the tonic D of the whole symphony. But with Bach it is the modulation itself, occurring between two distant keys, that matters most, not the functional relationship between those keys. Similar thinking seems to underlie the Fantasias H. 277 and 278 (*W. 58/6* and *58/7*), which have as their modulating goals contrasting middle sections in keys which are removed by a tritone and a half step, respectively, from the tonic of each piece.

Bach, after all, was capable of writing sonatas whose last movements end in a different key from the first. Actually, five such sonatas should be discounted; these consist of unconnected movements from the *Probestücke* (*W. 61/1-6*), where the choice of keys was a product of the works' pedagogic function. But the fourth sonata of the set, H. 73 (*W. 63/4*), includes a slow movement (in free binary form) which opens in D and ends in F-sharp minor; the latter is a "tonic preparation" for the key of the third movement, also in F-sharp minor. A later sonata, H. 273 (*W. 58/2*), is more extreme, passing from G-minor at the end of the second movement to E in the third.[32] There is no intervening transition, and the first movement is in G. Despite a few brief moves in the second movement toward keys related to E, it is difficult to find anything which prepares the key of the last movement. E major there is simply an unprepared surprise, with no functional relationship to anything preceding, unless it is to serve as a sort of deceptive resolution of the half-cadence (in G-minor) which closes the second movement.

Ex. 6-24.   Sonata (1781), H. 273 *(W. 58/2),* transition to third movement.

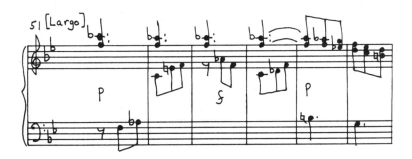

Ex. 6-24. (continued)

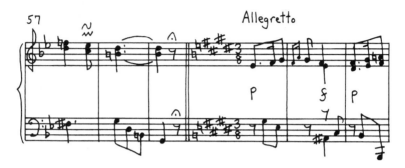

It is tempting to look for some explanation in the piece which immediately follows this sonata in the original publication *(Kenner und Liebhaber* IV, 1773). This is the Rondo in E, H. 274 (*W. 58-/3),* which comes to a halt in mm. 89-91 on a virtually unprepared G-minor chord, followed by an extended passage in that key. Both works date from 1781—the Rondo immediately precedes the Sonata in *NV*—and perhaps the two should be regarded as companion works, or even parts of a single composition.[33]

In such works the haze of local modulations obscures the larger functional relationships. There may be no logic to a series of tonicized areas except for that suggested by the chromatic voice-leading of the bass. Considering such pieces one wonders how essential is the tonal unity of the rondos and fantasias, which sometimes seem to return to their tonics as though by accident, having modulated without evident system or plan. Even in the sonata forms there often is no strong sense of a tonic/dominant (or any other) polarity; instead, there is a playing-out of various implications or continuations of the opening theme. Thus the work as a whole resembles a set of variations on a given type and ordering of material set down by the initial *Period.*

The limitations of this approach are obvious. Yet Bach's forms permit a wealth of fantastic detail, including various types of local contrast and discontinuity, which the more tightly organized forms of Haydn and Mozart can rarely countenance. It would be unfortunate to dismiss either the detail or the forms of Bach's music merely because they fail to conform to Classical expectations. On the other hand it is difficult not to regret the slightly tarnished brilliance of such works as the D-minor Concerto, H. 427 (*W. 23).* The concerto makes pretentions to a significant sort of drama in its expansive proportions and its gestures (see Example 6-18), and it indeed is dramatic, though never beyond a certain level close to the surface. By the same token, the proliferation of material or the rapid modulation in the solo keyboard works may lead one to regret the absence of greater control or economy in these aspects of composition. But in neither the concerto nor in even the most extreme fantasias or rondos does the music fail to cohere, in the sense that the music literally falls apart. The moment-to-moment continuity is usually clear enough, though music this involuted is particularly susceptible to incoherent *performances*. Perhaps some works fail to cohere in the sense that the sections hang together only loosely, and material heard at one point seems to have little to do with what is heard elsewhere in the piece. This possibility is strongest in the types of works discussed in the following chapter. But setting a standard of coherence is a subjective matter; from a purely analytic point of view, it is only possible to observe that Bach values a complex and ever-changing surface over a Classical unity of material or even of key. Hence it is somewhat irrelevant to inquire whether or not the works are coherent. As I suggested at the outset, my analyses might be understood as defining the standards which the works set for themselves, rather than as establishing coherence or incoherence absolutely.

7

Two Pieces *für Kenner und Liebhaber:* The Rondo in G, H. 268 (*W. 59/2*), and The Fantasia in C, H. 284 (*W. 59/6*)

The extraordinary late rondos and fantasias for solo keyboard are perhaps Bach's most characteristic pieces, and all the questions which his style raises are raised by them most forcibly. The works are distinguished by their freedom from the symmetrical forms and simple key structures of most other pieces, to which they add an extravagance of gesture and rhythmic freedom elsewhere confined to cadenzas and to transitions between movements. A comprehensive analysis of the two works named in the title is not the object here. Three questions, however might be elucidated:

1) What is the design of the work? Does the work possess a well-defined shape, and is the structure articulated through the same devices as in Bach's sonatas?
2) Do the many extraordinary events of these works have any deep structural significance, either as motives or as articulating devices, or are they employed only for their immediate effect?
3) Are the pieces coherent—or, rather, what sort of coherence obtains in these pieces? If a work is in some respects incoherent, is it therefore unsuccessful?

The sort of discussion demanded by these questions is necessarily of a detailed nature that does not make for the most gratifying reading. While some readers will want to skip over the more tedious passages of close analysis, to do so may be to overlook some of the "befindlicher Schönheiten" which Forkel found in music of this type.[1] Here, even more than in other works, Bach achieves his largest effects through the carefully calculated proliferation of many small ones, at least some of which must be analyzed in detail if the whole is to be properly evaluated.[2]

The Rondo in G, H. 268

The late rondos grow out of the simple type of rondo described toward the end of the preceding chapter. But even among the simpler examples are instances of what Kollmann called the "improper" rondo: works based not on several alternating themes but on a single principal theme stated in various keys, interspersed with free modulating passages.[3] Such a design resembles that of the concertos, and indeed Bach's rondos *für Kenner und Liebhaber* usually introduce passage-work and other virtuoso material, though the degree of virtuosity required is usually quite moderate (out of deference to the *Liebhaber*, one presumes). By contrast with the typical concerto movement, the key structure articulated by the statements of the rondo theme is so elaborate that Rosen rightly describes the form as "an improvised fantasy on one theme that wanders through several keys, with striking effects."[4] Yet the rondos differ from the fantasias in ways that go beyond their reliance on a returning theme; except in the D-minor Rondo, H. 290 (*W. 61/4*), the themes maintain a simple periodicity rare in the fantasias, and on the whole the rhythmic surface and the gestures of the rondos are comparatively straightforward, though hardly conventional.

In the *Kenner und Liebhaber* rondos it is useful to distinguish between what may be called *bridges*—relatively short, periodic passages which modulate or otherwise pass directly from one thematic statement to the next— and larger, more complex, *episodes* which may include rapid passage-work and any number of modulations to distantly related keys. To simplify the following discussion of the G-major Rondo, the form is summarized in the table below:

Table 7-1.   Structure of the Rondo in G, H. 268

measure number*	length in measures	key(s) tonicized	description
1	4+4	G	theme (antecedent, consequent)
9	4+4	G	theme varied
17	4	G-D:V	first bridge
21	4	D	theme (consequent phrase)
25	8	g-G:V	second bridge
33	8	G	theme varied
41	8	-f#:V	third bridge
49	8	f#-b	sequential repetition (from theme)
57	12	G	theme varied

Table 7.1 (continued)

69	25	b-C-b♭-a:V	first episode
94	8	F	theme varied
106	10	F-e	theme varied and extended
116	8	E	theme varied
124	24	g♯-A-g-g:V	second episode
148	8	-G:V	retransition
156	8	G	return: theme varied
164	4+6	G-G:V	theme varied and extended
174	11	G	coda (development of motives from theme)
185	4	G	closing phrase (from theme)

* In determining measure numbers, the six-beat measure at bar 31, marked *adagio,* has been counted as two measures, yielding a total of 188 measures in the piece.

The "keys tonicized" vary considerably with regard to their degree of confirmation, ranging from the solidly established dominant at measure 21 to the fleetingly established areas at measures 49, 69 and 124. This design results from a vast expansion of Bach's original version of rondo form, which is complete in the section of the piece up to bar 41, into something much larger. Because of the far-reaching modulations in the long central portions of the work (measures 69-155), the statement of the theme in the tonic at bar 156 takes on some of the character of the return in a sonata form. For this reason it seems appropriate to employ the terms used to describe the analogous points in a sonata form (retransition, return).

The shape of the piece is determined in part by the increasing length and animation of the successive modulating sections and the varied thematic reprises. Thus the figuration used to vary the third statement of the theme (at bar 33) foreshadows the passagework in the two episodes. The variation in the fourth thematic statement (measures 57-68), which expands each phrase of the theme through interpolation,[5] is the first departure from four-square periodic phrasing. Following this passage the piece enters into a more expansive, non-periodic type of rhythmic organization with the first episode. The group of thematic statements at the center of the piece (m. 94ff), and the long succession of passages in the tonic at the end (m. 156ff), each function as a single structural unit, alternating with and balancing the two large episodes. Thus the dimensions of the work grow as it moves forward; unlike the simple rondo forms described in Chapter 6, this one is asymmetrical. One or two statements of the theme at the end of the piece, while balancing the double period at the opening, would hardly have sufficed to offset the lengthy inner sections taken up by modulations far from the tonic. Hence, in addition to an expanded repetition of the theme, the closing passages include the climactic approach to a I6/+-chord at bar 177, suggestive of a cadenza; indeed a written-out cadenza occurs at the corresponding point in the Rondo in B-flat H. 267 (*W. 58/5*).

The opening parts of the piece and the final section in the tonic are relatively straightforward; odd things begin to happen in what I call the third bridge passage (m. 41ff). The opening two measures of the passage, bars 41-42, suggest a modulation toward A minor before the phrase turns enharmonically toward F-sharp in the following two bars. The latter are played *piano*, deepening the mysterious effect of the enharmonic re-interpretation of the chord. The end of the passage (measures 55-56) leads back to the theme through passing chromatic motion in the upper part(s), implying either some sort of deceptive resolution to G major or, as sketched below, an odd re-interpretation of the foreground voice-leading in the first measure of the theme.[6]

Ex. 7-1.   Rondo in G (1779), H. 268 *(W. 59/2).* Alternate
            sketches for mm. 55-58.

When the theme returns at bar 57, it is as if the preceding passage has been only an aberration and normal key relations are now to be resumed; there is little sense of continuity between bar 57 and what has just passed. But the first episode opens with an immediate move back to the key (B minor) left so abruptly in bars 55-6. In the succeeding flurry of modulations, both B minor and the original tonic (G) are soon forgotten, but there is little question that the first episode represents a resumption of the fantasia-like modulating process introduced in the third bridge.

The episode continues toward a passage of *arpeggiando* figuration later recapitulated in full. The restatement, in the second episode, is not quite literal: a single change in harmony (compare mm. 84 and 139) radically alters the tonal direction of the second episode, so that while the first episode as a whole modulates through a whole step from B minor to A minor, the second episode descends through only a half-step, from G-sharp minor to G minor.

As in so many of Bach's recapitulated passages, the change in tonal design is made as unnoticeable as possible; despite its dramatic surface, the passage as a whole is an essentially static block, and the alteration of the tonal scheme in the second appearance of the passage is not marked in any way. The motion generated by the passage-work dissolves at the end of the first episode (prior to the re-entrance of the rondo theme) in the empty measure at bar 93.[7] The parallel passage at the end of the second episode, though not quite coming to a full stop, leads into an eight-measure sequence which, like most retransitions in the sonatas, is rhythmically weak, almost superfluous. Yet by prolonging the dominant reached at the end of the second episode (m. 145), the retransition strengthens the sense of arrival at the restatement of the rondo theme in the tonic at bar 156. In addition, the last two bars of the retransition recall the *adagio* measure—a written-out *ritardando* containing six beats— which precedes an earlier return of the theme (at bar 33).

Neither the succession of keys in the two episodes nor the tonal design of the two central statements of the theme (at bars 94 and 116) submits to functional tonal analysis. For example, F major at bar 94 can hardly be heard as a Neapolitan to E at bar 116, since the intervening passages effectively obscure all tonal relations. E major is reached through a non-sequitur, a German-sixth chord which resolves directly to the tonic (and in a completely different register). Similar observations apply to the second episode, which even manages to land squarely on the tonic minor (at bar 137) without the slightest suggestion that this is anything more than one further step in the recapitulation of the errant modulations of the first episode.

This last observation is not intended as a derogatory criticism; it merely indicates that the tonal design is not dictated by considerations of harmonic function. In fact the piece has a tendency to modulate by half-step, regardless of functional relationships. B minor, which opens the first episode at bar 69, is shortly followed by C (bar 78) and B-flat minor (bar 82). Likewise the thematic statement in F (measure 94) is succeeded—at some distance, but with an opening in a comparable register and dynamic—by one in E (bar 116). The purpose of this is to bring distant key areas into close juxtaposition, as already occurred at the head of the third bridge. While hardly establishing a compelling logic for all the progressions, sudden modulation to a key related by half-step is the common element linking the sudden collisions of key areas *within* the episodes—especially in the passage-work at bars 84 and 139—with the larger design governing the succession of thematic statements in F and E.

Is there any stronger organizing factor beside the general one of swift modulation between distant keys? There are no obvious voice-leading connections linking the different sections, although a few significant chords— e.g., the diminished chord at bars 72 and 112, or another pair of similarly articulated diminished chords at bars 41 and 91—turn up prominently in scattered parts of the piece, suggesting the possibility of a different type of long-range connection, a possibility raised more pressingly in the Fantasia. Within each of the two episodes the linear bass imparts a certain sense of direction. But even this does not establish a sense of logical necessity in the succession of keys, for while each episode is built over a fairly simple chromatic bass line, as shown below, the line is too complicated to be reduced to a straightforward descent or some other equally cogent pattern.

Ex. 7-2.   Rondo in G. Figured bass sketch for the first episode, mm. 69-95.

As in other works, this bass line establishes a measure-to-measure continuity without articulating any higher level of organization. As in the E-minor sonata (Ex. 6-7a), a few plateaus of harmonic stability stand out for a few measures at a time, but in the course of this passage there is a gradual change in the character of the figuration and modulation; both increase in velocity, and with the onset of passage-work the modulations become swift and intensely chromatic. This effect is not unknown in the nineteenth century; the composer's concern is with the fact of the modulation itself, not the keys which are tonicized. It is enough to recognize that the key in m. 82 is quite distant from that at bar 73. Both keys call forth statements of the principal theme, and as in the E-minor sonata the effect of the closely juxtaposed thematic statements is to emphasize the sharp tonal contrast between them.

The first episode, however, goes beyond the middle section of that sonata; it marks the abandonment of the formal symmetry and homogeneity of texture that characterize Bach's sonata forms. Nor is the episode a mere interpolation placed between two structurally significant sections; in the course of the episode it becomes clear that it, not the recurring thematic statements, has become the true focus of the work. While the sonatas contain their share of individual events resembling those of the episode, none employ the long-range *processes* at work in the rondo, most notably the progressive heightening of tension within the individual sections and in the design of the work as a whole. Of course the recapitulation of the entire episode at bar 124 shows that Bach has not abandoned his architectonic conception of form; he still feels a need to contain the drama of the episodes within a symmetrical structure. But this symmetry is inexact, since the two episodes both lie toward the latter end of the work, which consequently takes on a considerably altered character in its later sections. The change in character comes about partly through the greater length of the individual sections, partly through the increasing arbitrariness of the tonal design. The latter has a curious and profound effect. The return emerges from the chaotic second episode with a quality quite different from that of the return in a sonata form; it represents a sudden shift back to the periodic simplicity of the rondo theme, which has been gradually abandoned in the course of the preceding sections. So dramatic a stroke, even if somewhat mitigated by the retransition phrase, is impossible within the homogeneous rhythmic and tonal procedures of Bach's sonata forms.

The Fantasia in C, H. 284

While most of the late rondos share the general shape of H. 268, no such consistency is found among the fantasias. To be sure, the big fantasias of the later period are, like the rondos, descended from smaller, simpler pieces written earlier in Bach's career. Several of the late fantasias open with the *arpeggiando* improvisation which furnishes the complete substance of some of the earlier fantasias. Beyond that, however, a very loose three-part form is the only common structural device. In one fantasia this produces a rough approximation of three-part sonata form—in the Fantasia in B-flat, H. 289 (*W. 61/3*). In several others the structure is closer to Da Capo form, framing a lyrical passage in strict time between rhythmically free outer sections employing similar material. The two fantasias of the fourth *Kenner und Liebhaber* set are of this type, while the Fantasia in C, from the fifth set, uses a modification of this design. As with the Rondo in G, it will be helpful to present a table showing the work's main sections and their keys:

Table 7-2. Structure of the Fantasia in C, H. 284.

measure* number	timing** minutes: seconds	keys tonicized	principal motive(s)	section and tempo	
1	0:00	C-G	a	A section:	Andantino	
9		G-a-f#-G:V	a	Andantino	
19	0:57	a#(bb)-F#-g	passage-work	Prestissimo	
31		g:I6/4	a	Andantino	
33	1:17	g#(ab)-a#(bb)-c#(db)-b	—	Andantino	
45		e:V	a	Andantino	
53	2:14	e	b	B section:	Allegretto	first part
69		e	b	Allegretto	first part varied and interpolated
90		-C	b	Allegretto	second part
102		C	b	Allegretto	extension (broken off)
106	3:18	-a, g#(ab)-d:I6/4	c	Transition:	Andantino	
112		d-c:I6/4	b	Allegretto	
120		c-c#:V	a, c	Andantino	
127		c#-d:V	b	Allegretto	
139	4:37	g-b-C:V	a	A' section:	Andantino	
147	5:00	B-C-d-e	passage-work	Prestissimo	
159	5:11	f-b-d:V	a, c	Andantino	
170	5:55	C	a	Andantino	

*The measure numbers given here were determined by assuming common time in the unbarred sections of the piece (on which see *Versuch*, vol. 2, p. 326), except in the two *prestissimo* passages, where 2/4 time was assumed. This yields a total of 180 measures in the piece.
**This column indicates the points in real time at which significant divisions of the work occurred in a performance by the author (total duration, 6 minutes, 26 seconds).

In contrast with the two fantasias of the 1783 set, the Da Capo form of this work is rendered ambiguous by the absence of a clear articulation marking the end of the B Section or the beginning of the A' section. The B section—the Allegretto beginning at bar 53—is in a truncated ternary form which breaks off shortly after reaching the second cadence (bar 101). From that point until bar 139 this Fantasia introduces a transitional section in which statements of the lyrical theme of the central Allegretto are interspersed with fragments of free writing in the opening tempo. Only at bar 139 does material from the first A section begin to reappear, not in the tonic, as it would in a sonata form or an ordinary Da Capo form, but in G minor, the minor dominant. Subsequently, the A' section restates most of the material of the first section in its original order, though in completely different harmonic contexts and without any reference to the *cantabile* passage beginning at bar 33.

The outer unbarred sections are remarkable among Bach's free fantasias for their dependence on just two chief motives, both based on upward arpeggiation, which are labeled *a* and *c* in Table 7-2. The first of these is the more imporant; motive *c* is introduced briefly at measure 17 but achieves prominence in the transition passages following the B section. The *a* motive, on the other hand, opens the work and is the only idea in the free sections whose role approaches that of the principal theme in Bach's other works, that is, to articulate plateaus in the tonal design.

But this fantasia, like all the larger free fantasias, differs from the rondos and other works in the brevity of the tonal plateaus, which even at the beginning and end are rarely more than a few measures in length. Indeed, except in the B section, the work is continuously in the state of harmonic flux reserved for the two long episodes of the rondo and for transition passages elsewhere. Where the rondo makes several opening excursions which return immediately to the tonic, the fantasia moves from C after only eight measures, not returning until the middle of the last page.[8] Moreover, the extraordinary number of harmonic elisions, fragmentary phrases, and like procedures in the fantasia create a far more complicated sort of continuity than in the rondo, where such disruptions of the surface are confined largely to the articulations between sections.

The many breaks in the surface continuity and the sudden juxtapositions of distant key areas themselves suggest an analytic approach to the fantasia. As in any work of Bach's there are various connections and lines in the fore- and middle-grounds, especially in the bass, that maintain the continuity over the interruptions of the surface. For example, a line beginning with d''' in measure 139 continues, after the *prestissimo* passage in measures 147-158, through a scalar descent and leads to the d'' of measure 170. (Ex. 7-3) There seem to be no deeper contrapuntal structures nor any simple funtional tonal design governing the whole. The coherence of the work depends largely on an

Ex. 7-3.   Fantasia in C (1784), H. 284 *(W. 59/6)*. Sketch of mm.
            139-80.

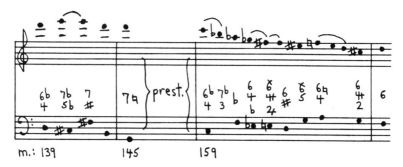

interlocking series of voice-leading connections and lines at levels close to the
surface.

To take one example of this sort of coherence, measures 31-33 are held
together by the chromatic voice-leading of the bass (c#-d-d♭-c♭), measures 33-44
by the retention of d♭″ (c#″) in the treble.

Ex. 7-4.   Fantasia in C. Sketch of mm. 31-44.

In other words, bar 33 is the point at which the preceding passage, held together
by the chromatic bass, links up with a passage based on the prolongation of
d-flat (c-sharp) in the upper register. Other than this—the termination of the
chromatic bass and the first appearance of the treble d-flat in the same
measure—there is no obvious connection between the two successive passages.
Hence the modulation from G minor to A-flat minor is as disorienting as the
similar half-step modulations in the rondo.

But there are other types of connection which hold certain parts of the
piece together. For instance, measures 31-32 connect back to bars 17-18 as a
resumption of the harmony G: V. The term "resumption" is used advisedly. The
Schenkerian expression "prolongation" would imply that the material
"prolongating" the G:V harmony is in some sense a diminution of it. But it is

not; the *prestissimo* passage is an interruption, a non-sequitur, and it does not "reduce" to (is not "generated" by) G:V. Thus the connection between bars 17-18 and bars 31-32 is different from the connection between bars 35 and 44; the latter connection is the product of the on-going retention of the note d-flat (c-sharp) in the treble. The segment of the work which embraces the *prestissimo* passage, on the other hand, is not organic or hierarchic in the same sense as the *cantabile* passage, and consequently its coherence must depend on something else.

That something else is a formal sense that the interrupting material will eventually be abandoned and a return of some sort made to whatever preceded the interruption.[9] In a more conventional piece one takes for granted this sort of formal connection, even though the same principal accounts for the coherence of a rondo or Da Capo form. Here the interruptions take the nature of non-sequiturs; their rhythmic and motivic content has little to do with the passages which they interrupt, and they are prepared and then abandoned through deceptive cadences or otherwise irregular voice-leading. Such practices stretch the idea of formal connection—the sense of continuity when a particular thematic idea, tempo, texture, or, as at bar 31, a harmony returns after some period of absence—to its limits. The formal connections also become entangled with one another: in the transition between the B and A' sections, which are the interrupting passages, those played Andantino, using the *a* and *c* motives, or those using the *b* motive and played Allegretto?

Actually there is no need to ask such a question. The passages in the transition establish a continuity which depends on the alternation of contrasting characters or motivic ideas.[10] One must attend simultaneously to two different processes: the half-step movement from the first Allegretto in D minor (bar 112) to the second Allegretto in C-sharp minor (bar 127), and the continuation at bar 120 and at bar 139 of the Andantino arpeggiation first heard in measures 106-111.

Perhaps this sort of continuity—the formal connection between passages separated from one another by intervening measures—can even be sensed between single chords widely separated from one another. (This possibility was raised earlier with regard to a few strikingly articulated diminished chords in the rondo.) The two Allegretto passages in the transition section are both prepared by the same diminished chord, heard initially in measure 110 as a pivot between E major and D minor. There the chord is even written as though it were meant to function as dominant of C-sharp, which it eventually does when it is heard again at bar 126. But when the chord resolves at bar 111 the e-sharp is reinterpreted as f-natural, producing a sudden shift to D minor. While the voice-leading which accomplishes this is faultless, the functional harmonic progression from measure 110 to 111 is less clear; one must understand the diminished chord as d:V/V, its resolution delayed until bar 115. If understood as C♯: V, the chord's resolution is even further delayed (until bar

127). Like the diminished chord which precedes the *prestissimo* passage,[11] this one establishes a connection between non-contiguous segments of the piece by resolving twice, as it were, once to an unexpected key and later to the one originally prepared.

A similar sort of connection is made by the chord heard in measure 120. This harmony stands out not only because of its arpeggiation through motive *a*, but also as a result of the concurrent return of the Andantino tempo. The chord is heard again near the end of the piece (bar 175), again articulated by the *a* motive. On its first appearance the chord functions as an enharmonic pivot between C and C-sharp . Later it is treated as a German-sixth, resolving to C: I$_{6/4}$ and thereby providing the final confirmation of C as tonic of the work. Thus the "second" resolution of the chord at bar 176 in a sense completes the modulation interrupted at bar 121.

Formal connections between isolated chords or motives would not in themselves establish the coherence of the work. But they combine with the suggestions of a sonata-style reprise in the final section to bring the work to a satisfying conclusion in the tonic. Still, in the transition section and in the more mysterious parts of the outer sections the form is, essentially, little more than one thing after another. This remains true even when the successive events refer back in a subtle and beautiful manner to previously heard events, through either harmony or motive or through both. The nature of the phrasing and of the events themselves tends to isolate the individual gestures as static events, analogous to the static formal sections or blocks of the rondo, but far shorter and more fragmentary.

The discontinuous motion—what might be called progression by non-sequitur—continues right up to bars 175-176, where the German-sixth first touched upon in bar 120 resolves to I$_{6/4}$. The passage is so powerful in part because it presents one of the few confirmations of any modulation. The "first" resolution of the chord, at bar 121, is part of a series of distant modulations to keys none of which is strongly established. Indeed, except for G major at measure 9 and E minor at the beginning of the B section, none of the keys tonicized in the piece is fully confirmed; like the Rondo, this piece undergoes a change of character when it finally moves out of hazily defined tonal areas and into a firm C major. A remarkable aspect of the closing section is its gradual restoration of cogent functional relationships between successive tonicizations.[12] The G-major harmony at bar 146 and the F minor tonicized at bar 158 function as dominant and sub-dominant, respectively, although, because of the piece's incessant wandering, the functionality of these harmonies is only clear in retrospect, beginning at measure 170. At that point D minor, which has been momentarily tonicized, becomes redefined as C: ii through its use in a diatonic sequence in C major. This passage, the only diatonic sequence in the piece, resembles the retransition of the Rondo analyzed above in indicating that, with the recovery of the tonic, the piece also returns to relatively conventional phrasing.

Clearly the rondo and the fantasia operate on similar principles—a linear foreground continuity is maintained in the face of numerous discontinuities in the articulated rhythm and arbitrary lurches in the tonal direction. That is to say that the works lack the strongly hierarchic organization of a Classical sonata form, or even of Bach's sonata form. In the latter the phrases, groups of phrases, and the two or three principal sections comprise a whole in which each part has a well-defined function in articulating the tonal design and—at least in the opening and closing phrases or each section—in presenting the motivic material. Hierarchic organization of this sort—which is greatly elaborated in the Classical style through the subdivision of the sections— insures a type of coherence which can easily be understood as being the *only* type of coherence possible in a musical work. Yet Bach's rondos and fantasias do cohere at the foreground, and, once their manner of progressing by non-sequitur is understood, little in them seems completely improbable or incongruous.

The absence of a strong tonic/dominant polarity, the emphasis on superficial detail, and the concentration of the elements of continuity—lines and connection—close to the surface are all characteristics which the rondos and fantasias share with Bach's other works. But the rondos and fantasias illustrate what Bach could do when not confined to his somewhat stilted version of sonata form: the discovery of relatively long-range processes in the rondos and of unconventional continuities in the fantasias. In this Bach shows a peculiar relationship with the Romantics, whose failure (or refusal) to comprehend Classical sonata form is well known. Schumann, Liszt, Chopin, and others of their generation largely avoided sonata form except in somewhat academic guises or in highly idiosyncratic transformations. They seem to have been conscious of the constraints it placed on their imagination and compositional freedom. Perhaps Bach was too, but as a composer he happily accepted those constraints. He may have routinely abandoned them in his improvisations, but before his later years it seems never to have occurred to him to set his improvisations down on paper—a few relatively brief pedagogic examples excepted, notably the so-called Hamlet fantasia from the *Probestücke* (*W. 63*). In his reluctance to compose in a style resembling that of improvisation (except at the surface), Bach resembles the Classical composers, especially Beethoven, who left very few works in a genuinely improvisational style. But when Bach finally did embrace improvisational genres it represented more than a simple desire to preserve a few improvisations for his admirers.[13] Bach's serious interest late in life in forms inspired by improvisation is remarkable—it produced more compositions and left more marks on his works in strict forms than in the case of, say, Friedemann Bach, in whom a similar interest might be detected. This interest in improvisation is, of course, another point of contact with the Romantics— perhaps the only one, in fact, which is manifest in Bach's actual forms and treatment of material.

8

A Critical Verdict

The late rondos and fantasias present the peculiarities of Bach's style—both strengths and weaknesses—in their purest and most concentrated form. That style, distilled and refined during Bach's fifty-odd years as a composer, performer, and improviser, had naturally undergone significant changes, particularly in Bach's increasing willingness to disrupt the surface through breaks in the texture, and in his increasing tendency to treat the entire composition, whether a single-movement keyboard fantasia or rondo or a multi-movement cycle, as a continuous succession of modulations and affects. Yet despite the increasing acceptance of improvisatory devices—"Fantasie"— into composition, even in his late works Bach rarely overstepped the essential bounds of a style which he had mastered by the early 1740's.

The manneristic style which characterizes all of his mature works is common to much of the music of the Berlin circle, above all the sonatas and fantasias of Friedemann Bach and Gottfried Müthel. Indeed, Friedemann probably outdoes Emanuel in striking disruptions of the continuity and in complex elaborations of simple formal designs. Müthel's florid embellishment of both treble and bass in many works goes beyond anything in Emanuel Bach. Emanuel's music is greater, however, for in it the striking or disturbing events are integrated into a whole which is far more cogent than in the music of the other North German mannerists. The bizarre events of some of the rondos and fantasias hide the fact that the proportions of these works are quite carefully worked out, though usually not according to the norms of Bach's sonata form. Many works, particularly the late ones, stretch the continuity to just short of the breaking point—a work such as the C-major Fantasia discussed in Chapter 7 is clearly calculated to come as close to incoherence as possible—but the expressive value of this flirtation with disaster would be lost if the music did not ultimately recoup itself and tie up some of the threads left hanging by the more discontinuous passages.

The near-incoherence of such a work must stem from a deliberate effort either to disorient the listener or to create a dramatic instrumental idiom analogous to serious opera and oratorio. In the former case, Bach would not be unlike the Mannerist painters of the sixteenth century in their efforts to confuse perspective or contradict traditional symmetries. In the latter case, Bach would be following an impulse arising from what Schering called the *redende Prinzip*, expressed most literally in the occasional examples of instrumental recitative. Both explanations certainly apply, and the underlying esthetic motivations seem clear: in part, the manneristic fascination with virtuosity and cleverness emphasized by Berg, but, more importantly, the aspiration toward direct personal expression. The latter brings Bach close to the Romantics, at least in his expressive goals, but Bach's continuing attachment to strict forms and traditional compositional methods suggests a more precise analogy to Beethoven, especially late Beethoven.

In two respects in particular, Bach's style seems to emerge as a response to expressive aspirations resembling those of Beethoven in his later works. Bach's almost compulsive tendency to avoid literal repetition and to eschew periodic phrasing springs from an attempt to render every moment of a work as intensely expressive as possible. The same impulse can be detected in the more concentrated pieces of Beethoven's late period, where it leads to a concision and an occasional eccentricity of phrasing not unlike those of Bach's Hamburg symphonies and sonatas. As I have already suggested, Beethoven's concern—particularly in the late quartets—with the cycle as a unified, continuous, composition, also has a precedent in Bach's Hamburg works (and in a few earlier ones). Despite the overwhelming sentiment of isolated moments in late Beethoven, the style remains essentially Classical; with Bach an equally high dosage of sentiment remains under the control of an aesthetic that valued symmetry at the largest level of form, and which, therefore, was best at representing expressive situations rather than carrying out dramatic processes.

Expression for Bach, as for other members of his generation, is conceived as the evocation of a particular affect through the character of the melodic surface or harmony. One basic affect applies over the course of an entire movement—a principle central to the aesthetics of a writer as late as Forkel—and thus in the rare cases where Bach seeks a genuine contrast of affect he usually achieves it through discontinuity: a break in the harmonic rhythm, a sudden change of tempo or texture, or some similar means. The continuous cyclic works and the improvisatory works for solo keyboard from the Hamburg period represent Bach's solution to the problem of depicting change or progression of affect in music. It is not entirely successful, if by success one means the elimination of the formality and symmetry inherent in Bach's forms. These remain, and even in such highly dramatic works as the B-minor Symphony (H. 661) or the F-minor Sonata (H. 173) it is clear that Bach's conception of drama remains that of late Baroque *opera seria*, not that of the Viennese Classical sonata or the Mozartean *opera buffa*.

One might accept with equanimity the relativistic judgement that one type of drama is as good as another, when considered on its own terms, if there were not signs that Bach occasionally aspired to a type of drama which his style simply could not attain, at least not without stretching its basic assumptions, as in the late rondos and fantasias. The attempt to create a dramatic return in the first movement of the F-minor sonata (see Ex. 6-9) is only partially successful, since the modulation is too direct and the tension generated by the move to F-flat is too quickly dissipated. In the D-minor concerto (H. 427) the work's self-consciously dramatic affect[1] is diffused by the somewhat rambling outer movements, especially in their lengthy recapitulations of passage-work—a characteristic shared with the rondos *für Kenner und Liebhaber*. It would be a mistake, however, to identify Bach's expressive aspirations in such works with those of a later generation. Bach's conception of expression, like his compositional technique, is manneristic: any unresolved tensions or apparent contradictions in his music may themselves be elements in a manneristic expressive design.

For example, in his approach to melodic embellishment Bach seems to subscribe to the ancient tradition of leaving ornamentation to the improvisation of the performer. Yet in the *Versuch* he grants this license only to experienced and insightful musicians,[2] and in his habit of incorporating written-out embellishments into revised versions of his works he far surpasses his father. Though any work remains susceptible to further embellishment, at any given stage of a work the melodic ornamentation is crystallized, not spontaneous—carefully written down and usually maintained in parallel passages in Bach's sonata-form movements. Indeed, one of the greatest paradoxes of the eighteenth century is that Emanuel Bach, the chief composer of the *Empfindsamkeit,* should have composed most of his music within a rigid sonata form. The most telling symbol of this is the first movement of the sixth Württemberg sonata, H. 36 (*W. 49/6*). Although its agitated harmony and halting phrasing render it the keyboard equivalent of a dramatic accompanied recitative, the dramatic effect requires a sensitive performer to sustain it as it recurs, without relief, through all three sections of a ternary sonata form with retransition. The paradox is even greater when both repeats are played (as they should be), especially with the composer's embellishments.[3]

But the inevitable tension between expressive, arbitrary, detail and, regular symmetrical form is itself an essential element of Bach's style, as in all manneristic styles. Both elements occur in his father's music, but with sufficient restraint and fluidity that the works remain untouched by mannerism—though in some works Sebastian comes very close, as in the Goldberg Variations. Sebastian Bach avoids mannerism through his generosity: no one aspect, such as harmony or melodic embellishment, is so exclusively the object of his attention as to bar him from applying his ingenuity to other elements of composition or to the balance between them. The florid melodic embellishment and chromatic harmony of the twenty-fifth of the Goldberg Variations occur within a framework defined by the two lower voices moving in simple double counterpoint; the embellishment of the upper line is carried out through a limited number of motives which are abandoned only at moments of particular intensity (especially the very end). Emanuel's music seeks such intensity at nearly every moment, through concentration on such single factors as the rhetorical articulation of the melody or the violent alternation of keys and textures. The result may be surprise when one discovers that the melody remains (as in the Goldberg Variations) an elaborate "variation" of a simple harmonic progression, the juxtaposed affects a series of parentheses within a simple sonata form. Such surprises rarely occur with Sebastian Bach.

Emanuel's music elicits such surprise—and raises corresponding questions—for a legitimate expressive purpose: to introduce a type of agitation, both emotional and intellectual, not found in Baroque or Classical music. The reverse side of this agitation is wit, and Emanuel's best effects are both passionate and witty, as when he opens a particularly *emfindsam* sonata, H. 243 (*W. 55/5*),in the wrong key. The arbitrariness of such a procedure will render it pale, to Classically oriented listeners, by comparison with Haydn's more purposeful deceptions. Yet Emanuel's intense concentration on a moment of exquisite illusion is as impossible in Haydn's style as Haydn's more broadly ranging humor is in Emanuel's. Few listeners will be as deeply moved by Emanuel's music as they are by the best works of his father or of the Viennese Classical composers. The ultimate preference of most listeners for those styles is a powerful but perhaps an arbitrary one, based on deeply engrained and, in a general sense, classical, artistic ideals. Emanuel Bach's music proceeds from quite different principles, but nonetheless follows a consistent logic. The choice of liking or disliking each work is another matter.

Notes

Chapter 1

1. *The Classical Style* (New York: Norton, 1971), p. 44.

2. Ibid., p. 19.

3. Jan LaRue, *Guidelines for Style Analysis* (New York: Norton, 1970), p. 121, referring to "style stratification" in a Sinfonia by Leopold Mozart. For an analysis of the questionable historiography underlying this concept, see Carl Dahlhaus, *Fundamentals of Music History*, trans. J. B. Robinson (London: Cambridge University Press, 1983), pp. 14 ff.

4. Philip Trevelyan Barford, "The Sonata Principle: A Study of Musical Thought in the Eighteenth Century," *Music Review* 13 (1952): 262. The quotation from Tovey is not further identified, and I have been unable to locate it in his works.

5. Jan LaRue, "Symphonie," *MGG* XII: 1830.

6. *The Classical Style*, p. 115.

7. *Thematic Catalog of the Works of Carl Philipp Emanuel Bach* (in press). The work-list included in Helm's article on C.P.E. Bach in *New Grove* I:855-62 is an abstract of the *Catalog* and includes a collation of the *HV* and *WV* numbering systems. Rachel Wade traces the history of the catalogs, up to and including *WV*, in *The Keyboard Concertos of Carl Philipp Emanuel Bach*, in Studies in Musicology, ed. George Buelow, vol. 48 (Ann Arbor: UMI Research Press, 1981), pp. 5-14. The abstract of *HV* in *New Grove* must be used with caution, as it contains a number of typographical errors.

8. The so-called *Nachlassverzeichnis* (Hamburg, 1790) has been published in modern edition by Heinrich Miesner, in *BJ* 35 (1938): 103-36 and 36 (1939): 81-112, and in facsimile (Ann Arbor: University Microfilms, 1976).

9. Paul Kast, *Die Bach-Handschriften der Berliner Staatsbibliothek*, Tübinger Bach-Studien, ed. Walter Gerstenberg, Heft 2/3 (Trossingen: Hohner, 1958), pp. 112-3. A number of the works attributed to C.P.E. Bach in this list are inauthentic; a number of others are in fact alternate versions of pieces included in *WV*.

10. Letter, Bach to J.J. Eschenburg (January 21, 1786), ed. and trans. Dragan Plamenac, "New Light on the Last Years of Carl Philipp Emanuel Bach," *MQ* 35 (1949): 585. Bach is amused that the King of England, George III, should have preserved even the youthful works of Händel, whose centenary had been recently and spectacularly observed.

11. See, for example, Wade's confirmation that the keyboard concerto published by Huberty (Paris, c. 1762) is the original version of H. 404 (*W. 2*), in *The Keyboard Concertos*, p. 25.

Chapter 2

1.   Dates are those given in *NV* unless otherwise noted.

2.   Though not officially in Frederick's service until the latter's accession to the throne in 1740, Bach evidently was associated with the Crown Prince from the time Bach left for Berlin in 1738; see C.H. Bitter, *Carl Philipp Emanuel und Wilhelm Friedemann Bach und deren Brüder* (Berlin, 1868; rpt. Leipzig: Zentralantiquariat der Deutschen Demokratischen Republik, 1973) I: 14-5, 19.

3.   See Heinrich Miesner, *Philipp Emanuel Bach in Hamburg* (Wiesbaden: Breitkopf und Härtel, 1929), pp. 60-7. Bach's Hamburg church music is the subject of a forthcoming Princeton University dissertation by Stephen Clark, "The Occasional Choral Works of C.P.E. Bach."

4.   Charles Burney's account of musical conditions at the Berlin court—dating, it is true, from after Bach's departure—occurs in *The Present State of Music in Germany, the Netherlands and the United Provinces* (London, 1775; rpt. New York: Broude, 1969), II: 91 ff.

5.   Darrell Matthews Berg, "The Keyboard Sonatas of C.P.E. Bach: An Expression of the Mannerist Principle," diss., State University of New York at Buffalo, 1975, pp. 95-6.

6.   Ibid., p. 101.

7.   These pieces are not necessarily portraits of "ladies in Bach's circle of Berlin friends," as Erwin R. Jacobi suggests in "Five Hitherto Unknown Letters from C.P.E. Bach to J.J.H. Westphal," *JAMS* 23 (1970): 121. Following the custom of the French and Italians, the gender of any piece is feminine. Thus *La Prinzette*, H. 90 (*W. 117/21*), refers to Prince Friedrich Wilhelm of Printzen, according to Heinrich Miesner, "Aus der Umwelt Philipp Emanuel Bachs," *BJ* 34 (1937): 135-6.

8.   Discussed by Bitter, I: 173-4. Wade, *The Keyboard Concertos*, p. 29, describes the care with which Bach evidently endeavored to leave his wife a "pension" after his death by withholding certain works from publication during his lifetime. But Joanna Maria herself should perhaps share the praise (or blame) for Back's commercial acumen; she came from a family of wine merchants and showed shrewd business sense in handling her husband's estate.

9.   Bach discusses the practice of varying the repeated sections of sonatas at the close of the first volume of his famous *Versuch über die wahre Art das Clavier zu spielen* (Berlin, 1753-62); rpt. ed. Lothar Hoffmann-Erbrecht (Leipzig: Breitkopf und Härtel, 1969); trans. William J. Mitchell as *Essay on the True Art of Playing Keyboard Instruments* (New York: Norton, 1949). H. 135 is practically identical with H. 133 (*W. 70/1*), the first of six *manualiter* organ sonatas.

10.   ". . . damit man nach meinem Tode sehen könne, welcher Fantast ich war." Letter to J.G.I. Breitkopf, October 15, 1782, quoted by Hermann von Hase, "Carl Philipp Emanuel Bach und Joh. Gottl. Im. Breitkopf," *BJ* 8 (1911): 97. This letter follows one of September 10 of the same year in which Bach says he has "escaped death" ("dem Tode entlaufen") after an illness which had delayed the composition of the set (W. 58) containing the fantasias in question.

11.   Called Quartets because of the written-out right-hand part for keyboard. E.F. Schmid's suggestion to add a cello (preface to his edition of the Quartets, 3 vols., Kassel: Bärenreiter, 1952) is plausible, considering the implicit doubling of the bass line by cello or gamba in earlier chamber music with obligato keyboard. But the designation as a quartet does not demand a fourth instrument—Bach's duos for keyboard and violin or flute are designated as trios in eighteenth-century sources, including *NV*—and the cello part supplied by Schmid in

his edition includes arbitrary decisions about where the cello should rest, play an octave below the left hand, or even double the viola part.

12.   Here and subsequently the terms "sonata" and "concerto" without further qualification will refer to works for keyboard.

13.   But the influence of Frederick the Great on the composition of flute works should not be assumed, as Bitter (I: 19) and later writers tend to do. Burney (*The Present State of Music in Germany*, II: 262-3) relates the King's active distaste for Bach and his music, at least in the later years of Bach's Berlin employment. Of course, the King's penchant for the flute would have been imitated in other Berlin circles in which Bach's music was better received.

14.   Rosen, in *The Classical Style*, pp. 367-8, makes a similar observation about the ability of the Viennese Classical composers to produce old-fashioned church music more or less in Baroque style.

15.   Bach's autobiography was inserted into the German translation, begun by C.D. Ebeling and completed by J.J.C. Bode, of Burney's *Present State of Music: Carl Burney's ... musikalische Reisen ... Dritter Band* (Hamburg, 1773; rpt. Kassel: Bärenreiter, 1959), p. 208. The autobiography has been translated by William S. Newman in "Emanuel Bach's Autobiography," *MQ* 51 (965): 363-72.

16.   Bach even wrote varied reprises for a set of variations whose theme is in binary form; hence the *Variationes mit veränderten Reprisen*, H. 259 (*W. 118/10*). As in many other works with varied reprises, Bach seems to have written the latter some time after the work's first composition. Although the autograph is apparently lost, the copy by J.J.H. Westphal conscientiously includes the signs   /   (Bach's indication for interpolated material) around each of the varied reprises (in *B Bc* U5899). A version of the work as a piano trio, H. 535 (*W. 91-4*), lacks the varied reprises, which were written out in the autograph of the trio (P 358) separately from the rest of the piece and without the string parts. Since Bach's preface to W. 91 mentions the possibility of performing the trios as keyboard solos, it is possible that Bach first arranged the work as a piano trio by adding the string accompaniment, and only afterwards wrote out the varied reprises. Another possibility is that the version as a piano trio is the original version, and Westphal's copy of the keyboard part is his own creation and should not be listed as a separate work.

17.   *Musicalische Reisen* III: 201.

18.   Thus Lessing quotes Bach's autobiography with approval before attacking the decline of popular taste, which Lessing attributes to the popularity of comic opera. *Kollektaneen zur Literatur*, ed. J.J. Eschenburg (Vienna, 1804) II: 245-6, quoted by Heinrich Miesner, *Philipp Emanuel Bach in Hamburg: Beiträge zu seiner Biographie und zur Musikgeschichte seiner Zeit* (Wiesbaden: Breitkopf und Härtel, 1929), pp. 37-8.

19.   The *Singspiel* was presented only in February, 1788, ten months before Emanuel's death, according to Otto Deutsch, *Mozart: A Documentary Biography*, 2d ed. (Stanford: Stanford University Press, 1966), p. 311. But apparently it was one of the works which Friedrich had brought back from London after his visit there in 1778.

20.   Miesner, *Bach in Hamburg*, p. 46.

21.   Quoted (without citation) by Karl Geiringer, *Joseph Haydn: A Creative Life in Music* (Berkeley and Los Angeles: University of California Press, 1968), p. 71. H.C. Robbins Landon repeats the quotation without locating the source in *Haydn: Chronicle and Works* (Bloomington: Indiana University Press, 1978) II: 393.

22.   Landon, II: 582.

23. See the letters to Forkel and A. Reinagle quoted by Peter Schleuning, *Die freie Fantasie: Ein Beitrag zur Erforschung der klassischen Klaviermusik* (Göppingen: Kümmerle, 1973), pp. 234-5. Bach assures Forkel that he has yet to write a concerto with a rondo finale—although several of the piano trios, composed at roughly the time of the letter (1775), conclude with rondos.

24. The Sinfonia, H. 508 (*W. 74*), and two sets of little pieces (W. 81 and 82) for keyboard with flute or violin. The keyboard fantasia entitled *C.P.E. Bachs Empfindungen*, one of the composer's most remarkable pieces, exists in a version to which Bach added a wholly subsidiary violin part as well as a second movement. This version is listed as H. 537 (*W. 80*).

25. He accepts at face value Bach's intimation to his publisher that, in the sonatas of W. 56, he "hopes for everyone" ("ich hoffe für Jedermann"), letter of November, 1779, to Breitkopf, in Hase, *BJ* 8 (1911): 96, quoted by Schleuning, p. 237 fn.

26. Schleuning, p. 236.

27. On the eighteenth-century distinction between *Kenner* and *Liebhaber*, see Erich Herbert Beurmann, "Die Klaviersonaten Carl Philipp Emanuel Bachs," Diss., Georg-August Universität (Göttingen), 1952 , pp. 78-80.

28. Rosen, *The Classical Style*, pp. 329-50; Landon, II: 345. Landon discusses Haydn's efforts to "reconcile his private musical thoughts with works for the broad public," something which Bach managed to do most successfully in his Hamburg publications.

29. *The Sonata in the Classic Era*, 2d ed. (New York: Norton, 1972), p. 119.

30. *Sonata Forms* (New York: Norton, 1980), p. 13.

31. For example, the two- or three-part texture characteristic of *galant* orchestral writing is common in Italian opera *sinfonie* and ritornelli from the early eighteenth century.

32. The dynamic markings found in Bach's early sonata publications are tabulated in Lothar Hoffmann-Erbrecht, "Sturm und Drang in der deutschen Klaviermusik von 1750-1763," *Musikforschung* 10 (1957): 470.

33. Beurmann, pp. 48-54, discusses the more or less simultaneous appearance of symphonic textures in the sonatas and of keyboard reductions of Bach's symphonies. The first of five such reductions, H. 45 (*W. 122/1*), dates from 1745 and is arranged from Bach's first symphony, H. 649 (W. 173). While one might question the reliability of *NV* with regard to the date of the keyboard version of the symphony, which appeared in 1741, in the apparent absence of any other information the date of the reduction (and its attribution to Bach) should probably stand.

34. Among them Newman; see *The Sonata in the Classic Era*, pp. 120-3, for a discussion along traditional lines of the historical importance of the galant style.

35. Berg, *The Keyboard Sonatas*, p. 90.

36. *Der critische Musicus* (Leipzig, 1737-40), pp. 128-9, quoted by David A. Sheldon, "The Galant Style Revisited and Re-evaluated," *Acta* 47 (1975): 259.

37. Sheldon, *Acta* 47: 243 ff.

38. Sheldon, *Acta* 47: 246; cf. Johann David Heinichen, "Von theatralischen Resolutionibus der Dissonantien," the opening chapter of Part 2 of his *Generalbass in der Komposition* (Dresden, 1728).

39.   J.J. Quantz, *Versuch einer Anweisung die Flöte traversiere zu spielen* (Berlin, 1752; rpt. of the 3d ed. (1789), Kassel: Bärenreiter, 1953), p. 302.

40.   *The Keyboard Sonatas*, pp. 10-11, 19.

41.   *Sonata in the Classic Era*, pp. 122-3.

42.   Landon II: 266-7.

43.   "Sturm und Drang," *Musikforschung* 10: 467.

44.   Rosen, "Bach and Handel," *Keyboard Music*, ed. Denis Matthews (New York: Praeger, 1972), p. 105.

45.   *The Classical Style*, p. 47.

46.   "Bach the Progressive," *MQ* 62 (1976): 328-42.

47.   *Sonata in the Classic Era*, p. 121.

48.   *Mannerism in Italian Music and Culture*, 1530-1630 (Chapel Hill: University of North Carolina Press, 1979).

49.   "Mannered Notation," *The Notation of Polyphonic Music*, 5th ed. (Cambridge, Mass.: The Mediaeval Academy of America, 1961), pp. 403-35.

50.   *French Secular Music of the Late Fourteenth Century* (Cambridge, Mass.: The Mediaeval Academy of America, 1950), p. 10b.

51.   Otto Vrieslander, *Carl Philipp Emanuel Bach* (Munich: Piper, 1923), quoted by Miesner, *Bach in Hamburg*, p. 113.

52.   *Bach in Hamburg*, p. 111.

53.   *Guidelines for Style Analysis* (New York: Norton, 1970), p. 121.

54.   In his autobiography Bach wrote, "In der Komposition und im Clavierspielen habe ich nie andern Lehrmeister gehabt, als meinen Vater," in *Musicalische Reisen*, III: 199.

55.   *Die Klaviersonaten*, pp. 36-7.

56.   *The Keyboard Sonatas*, p. 88

57.   Robert Lewis Marshall, *The Compositional Process of J.S. Bach: A Study of the Autograph Scores of the Vocal Works* (Princeton: Princeton University Press, 1972), I: 240.

58.   E.F. Schmid mentions Bach's "reverence" for the older composer, *Carl Philipp Emanuel Bach und seine Kammermusik* (Kassel: Bärenreiter, 1931), p. 32.

59.   A number of these works, including at least one cantata, slipped into the Schmieder thematic catalog and are now listed among the doubtful and misattributed works in *New Grove*.

60.   *Abhandlung von der Fuge* (Berlin, 1753; rpt., Hildesheim: Olms, 1970), I: 13, in reference to an excerpt from a trio by C.H. Graun reproduced in *Tabula* VI, fig. 1. Marpurg describes the example as an instance of *canonische Nachahmung*, but it is in fact a case of the pseudo-canonic sequence discussed in Chapter 4 (cf. Ex. 4-1).

61.   Jane Stevens, "The Keyboard Concertos of Carl Philipp Emanuel Bach," diss., Yale University, 1965, p. 13.

62.   Elizabeth Loretta Hays quotes the preface of Marpurg's *Die Kunst das Clavier zu spielen* (Berlin, 1750) to the effect that the "Bach's"—presumably Friedemann and Emanuel—esteemed

Couperin as "worthy of their acclamation," in the Commentary volume of her dissertation, "F.W. Marpurg's *Anleitung zum Clavierspielen* (Berlin, 1755) and *Principes du clavecin* (Berlin, 1756): Translation and Commentary," Stanford Univ., 1976, p. 71.

63. *MGG* VII: 1828.

64. See Burney, *The Present State of Music in Germany* II: 231-5, on Quantz and the Graun brothers at Berlin. All three musicians must have been among the visitors to Leipzig whom Emanuel would have met in his youth (see his autobiography, in *Musicalische Reisen* III: 201). Gottlieb Graun had a further connection with the Bach family as Friedemann's violin teacher; see Martin Falck, *Wilhelm Friedemann Bach: Sein Leben und seine Werke* (Leipzig: Kahnt, 1913), p. 8.

65. Shelley Davis includes several extensive quotations from Christian's Berlin concertos in "H.C. Koch, the Classic Concerto, and the Sonata-Form Retransition," *Journal of Musicology* 2 (1983): 45-61.

66. For an example from Haydn, see Landon II: 337-8.

67. Wade, *The Keyboard Concertos*, p. 53.

68. Reported by Johann Nicolaus Forkel, *Musicalischer Almanach für Deutschland auf das Jahr 1789* (Leipzig, 1789; rpt., Hildesheim: Olms, 1974), quoted (in translation) by Deutsch, pp. 310-11.

69. As did Arnold Schering, "Carl Philipp Emanuel Bach und das 'redende Prinzip' in der Musik, *Jahrbuch der Musikbibliothek Peters für 1937* (1938): 18 ff.

Chapter 3

1. Burney's oft-quoted account is in *The Present State of Music in Germany* II: 270-1.

2. *Essay*, trans. Mitchell, p. 152.

3. "nächst Gottes Ehre, das Vergnügen und die Bewegung der Zuhörer." Johann Mattheson, *Der vollkommene Capellmeister* (Hamburg, 1739; rpt. ed. Margarethe Riemann, Kassel: Bärenreiter, 1954), p. 129.

4. "eine Empfindung auf einem gewissen Punkte von Lebhaftigkeit," *Musicalischer Almanach für Deutschland auf das Jahr 1784* (Leipzig, 1784; rpt., Hildesheim: Olms, 1974), p. 25.

5. The original exchange of polemics between Scheibe and the Leipzig professor of rhetoric Johann Abraham Birnbaum, who defended Bach, took place in 1738 and is reproduced in *Bach-Dokumente, Band II. Fremdschriftliche und gedruckte Dokumente zur Lebens- geschichte Johann Sebastian Bachs 1685-1750*, ed. Werner Neumann and Hans-Joachim Schulze (Kassel: Bärenreiter, 1969), p. 304. Scheibe continued to criticize Bach, though not by name, in later writings, using the same terms as in the original criticism. The discussion of "musical metaphors" occurs in his *Critischer Musicus. Neue, vermehrte und verbesserte Auflage (Leipzig,* 1745), pp. 646-8.

6. E.g. the "Recensionen, Ankündigungen . . ." for the fourth set of pieces *für Kenner und Liebhaber* (W. 58), in Cramer's *Magazin der Musik* (Hamburg, 1783-4; rpt., Hildesheim: Olms, 1971) I/II: 1238-59.

7. In his review of the F-minor sonata H. 153 (*W. 56/6*) Forkel sets forth his view of the sonata cycle as the musical equivalent of the ode; successive movements present a progression of "ausdrucksvoller musicalischer Ideen," *Almanach für 1784*, p. 27.

8. These texts first appeared in Cramer's song collection *Flora, erste Sammlung* (Hamburg, 1787), and are edited and translated in E. Eugene Helm, "The 'Hamlet' Fantasy and the Literary Element in C.P.E. Bach's Music," *MQ* 58 (1972): 281-2.

9. *MQ* 58: 288.

10. "nur allgemeine Ideen vertragt." Letter to Friedrich Nicolai, cited by Schmid, p. 52.

11. "er Dinge mählte, welche Musik gar nicht mahlen sollte." *Kollektaneen zur Literatur* II: 202, quoted by Max Schneider, introduction to his edition of Telemann, *Der Tag des Gerichts* and *Ino*, in: *Denkmäler der deutscher Tonkunst* 28 (Leipzig, 1908): lvi fn.

12. Miesner, *Bach in Hamburg*, pp. 31-6, discusses Bach's relations with Lessing, Gerstenberg and others.

13. Schering, " 'redende Prinzip'," *Jahrbuch für 1937*: 23.

14. "The Keyboard Sonatas," pp. 206-8.

15. "Der Affekt ist nicht mehr Symbol, sondern gewinnt Realitätswert." "Die Klaviersonaten," p. 32.

16. "Allegory in Baroque Music," *Journal of the Warburg and Courtauld Institutes* 3 (1939-40): 21, 20.

17. Friedrich's letter of April 1, 1773, is quoted (in translation) by Helm, "The 'Hamlet' Fantasy," *MQ* 58 (1972): 291 fn, which also quotes Emanuel's letter in the main text. See also Schleuning, pp. 178-9.

18. As Peter Cohen attempts to do for the *Empfindugen* fantasia, H. 300 (*W. 67*), in *Theorie und Praxis der Clavierästhetik Carl Philipp Emanuel Bachs* (Hamburg: Wagner, 1974), pp. 188-90.

19. "Die Kunst der Improvisation," *Das Meisterwerk in der Musik* (Munich: Drei Masken, 1925-30) I: 12. Translation from Sylvan Kalib, "Thirteen Essays from the Three Yearbooks 'Das Meisterwerk in der Musik' by Heinrich Schenker," diss., University of Michigan, 1977, I: 5.

20. Ibid., p. 11 (translation from Kalib, I: 2).

21. *The Handleitung zur Variation* is the second volume of Niedt's *Musicalischer Handleitung*. The first volume, a figured bass treatise (and by far the best known volume in the work), appeared in 1700, while the third volume on counterpoint was published in 1717. I have discussed Niedt and his importance to eighteenth-century composition in "Composition as Variation: Inquiries into the Compositional Procedures of the Bach Circle of Composers," in *Current Musicology* 33 (1984).

22. *Musicalischer Handleitung . . . dritter und letzter Theil handlend vom Contra-Punct, Canon, Motteten...*(Hamburg, 1717).

23. Johann Philipp Kirnberger described J.S. Bach's teaching in *Gedanken über die verschiedenen Lehrarten in der Komposition als Vorbereitung zur Fugenkenntniss* (Vienna, 1782), pp. 4-5. Emanuel's comments on the subject are contained in a letter to Forkel quoted (in translation) in *The Bach Reader*, rev. ed., ed. Hans T. David and Arthur Mendel (New York: Norton, 1966), p. 279.

24. *Sonaten aus'm Ermel zu schüddeln* (Berlin, 1783). For a facsimile and translation, see Newman, "Kirnberger's 'Method for Tossing Off Sonatas'," *MQ* 47 (1961): 517-25. The translation only is reprinted in *The Sonata in the Classic Era*, pp. 442-3.

25. Partially transcribed by Newman, *MQ* 47: 517-25. Kirnberger's "method" is clearly related to two works of uncertain authorship (listed as BWV 1021 and 1038) which share bass lines with authentic works of J.S. Bach; see my "Composition as Variation."

26. *MQ* 47: 518.

27. "Es erhellet hieraus, dass in der heutigen Music der Bass die wichtigsten Parthie sey, welcher alle Stimmen untergeordnet sind . . . Wenn der Tonsetzer die Folge der Basstöne gut gewählt, und die Töne der obern Stimmen regelmässig daraus hergleitet hat, so ist der Satz rein." "Bass," *Allgemeine Theorie der schönen Kunst*, ed. Johann Georg Sulzer (Leipzig, 1792; rpt., Hildesheim: Olms, 1970), I: 298.

28. "die zur Ausziehrung dienenden Töne au der Harmonie der Hauptnote genommen." *Die Kunst des reinen Satzes* (Berlin and Königsberg, 1771-9; rpt., Hildesheim: Olms, 1968)I: 194-5. Bach's *Versuch*, II: 337, includes *Brechung mit Acciaturen* among the varieties of *Harpeggio* employed in improvisation.

29. "Man begreift, dass keine Melodie schön ist, die nicht gewisse Veränderungen der Haupt-noten, gewisse Zusätze, Verkleinerungen, Ausdehnungen, und andere scharfsinnige und bereits durchgehendes angenommene Zierrathen enthalte . . . Der verblühmte Ausdruck ist nämlich eine neue und zierliche Veränderung eines kurzen melodischer Satzes, um denselben nachdrücklicher, oder wohl gar erhabener zu machen, doch ohne Verletzung der Harmonie." *Der critische Musicus* (1745), p. 644.

30. Scheibe explicitly distinguishes the "verblühmte Ausdrucken" from the "Figuren in eigentlichen Verstande," Ibid., p. 644.

31. E.g. in the *Principes du clavecin* (Berlin, 1756; rpt., Geneva: Minkoff, 1974), p. 50. The *Principes* is a translation of the *Anleitung zum Clavierspielen* of the previous year (rpt. of the 2d ed. (Berlin, 1765), New York: Broude, 1969), with some important added material.

32. Beurmann, "Die Reprisensonaten Carl Philipp Emanuel Bachs," *Archiv für Musikwissenschaft* 13 (1956): 175-9.

33. "nachhero zweimal durchaus verändert." *NV*, ed. Miesner, *BJ* 35 (1938): 115.

34. The collection is preserved in P 1135 (mostly autograph) and in *B* Bc U5885 (J.J.H. Westphal).

35. Both versions of H. 18/2 are given in Berg, "The Keyboard Sonatas," pp. 359-62.

36. For instance, Bach added embellishments into the keyboard part in the autograph score (P 353) of the second movement of the concerto H. 478 (*W. 45*). In Michel's copy of the harpsichord part of the concerto H. 448 (*W. 37*)(St 526), Bach substituted more active figuration in several of the solo passages.

37. Wade, *The Keyboard Concertos*, pp. 96-7, shows that in this one case the embellished version (preserved in P 711, autograph score entitled *Auszierungen zum Adagio*) indeed documents Bach's actual performance. On the practice of embellishment in the Berlin style, see Quantz's *Versuch*, esp. "Von der Art das Adagio zu spielen," pp. 136-51.

38. Noted by Beurmann, *Archiv für Musikwissenschaft* 13: 178-9. In fact not every sonata with varied reprises maintains such parallelisms with absolute rigor; minor exceptions occur in the second *Reprise-Sonate*, H. 137 (*W. 50/2*) 1, and in Bach's ms. embellishments for the first movement of the sixth Württemberg Sonata H. 36 (*W. 49/6*), which are among those included in H. 164 (cf. Note 3-34).

39. "Von der Vortrag," I: 132-3.

40. *Anleitung*, p. 39. "In engerem Verstande aber versteht man durch *Figuren*, die Anwendung der Setzmanieren auf einem gewissen Affect oder Gegenstand, und werden solche mit gewissen aus der Rhetorik entlehen Namen beleget." The "stricter" sense of *Figuren* is distinguished from the free (*weitem*) usage which equates it with "ornament" (*Manier*).

41. Scheibe, *Der critische Musicus* (1731-40), p. 387, quoted in translation by Berg, "The Keyboard Sonatas," pp. 218-9.

42. "The Keyboard Sonatas," pp. 164-5.

43. This expression was applied to Bach's music "zu seiner Zeit" according to an anonymous review of the Variations H. 14 (*W. 118/7*), *Allgemeine musikalische Zeitung* 6/15 (January 11, 1804): 243-4.

44. "The Keyboard Sonatas," pp. 219-20.

45. See Fred Ritzel, *Die Entwicklung der "Sonatenform" im musik-theoretischen Schrifftum des 18. und 19. Jahrhunderts.*, 2d ed. (Wiesbaden: Breitkopf und Härtel, 1969), pp, 23 ff.

46. The following discussion draws principally on Marpurg's *Principes*, pp. 44-50 (containing discussions of form lacking in the German version), and Heinrich Christoph Koch, *Versuch einer Anleitung zur Composition* (Rudolstadt, 1782, and Berlin, 1787-93; rpt., Hildesheim: Olms, 1969). The latter, though late, contains much that refers directly to the style of Emanuel Bach and his fellow North Germans—more so than Koch's later *Musikalisches Lexikon* (Frankfurt, 1802; rpt., Hildesheim: Olm, 1964), which seems to reflect a stronger orientation toward the Viennese Classical style. An additional source, of some interest because it belongs to the pedagogic tradition of Marpurg's *Anleitung* and Bach's *Versuch*, is Georg Simon Löhlein's *Clavier-Schule* (Leipzig, 1765), I: 181-8.

47. *Kritische Briefe über die Tonkunst* (Berlin, 1759-64; rpt., Hildesheim: Olm, 1974) II: 4-5.

48. *Versuch* III: 346 ff.

49. Likewise Scheibe, *Critischer Musicus* (1745), pp. 623-4.

50. *Sonata Forms*, pp. 17-18. Rosen's discussion recalls the last two chapters of Koch's *Versuch*, which show how the brief *Perioden* of simple binary dance forms are expanded in the larger forms through the inclusion of numerous sub-sections.

51. *The Sonata in the Classic Era*, pp. 143-4. Newman's discussion should be read in light of Tovey's general introduction to the *Essays in Musical Analysis* (London: Oxford University Press, 1935), I: 10-11, which concludes that Classical sonata-allegro form, despite its three functional divisions, is essentially binary. Tovey notes that in no eighteenth-century sonata form can the middle section (development) be repeated apart from the final section (recapitulation). On the other hand, Tovey's position depends on Classical models in which a single tonic/dominant polarity prevails and in which the development is significantly different in form and function from the other sections. Neither condition obtains in the first movements of Bach's symphonies and concertos, which also lack double-bars at the center. Such movements illustrate the ternary principle at the heart of one variety of pre-Classical sonata form.

52. *Guidelines*, p. 187.

53. *Versuch* III: 310.

54. The Allegro, H. 337/2 (*W. 116/17*), analyzed in *Principes*, pp. 47-8. Marpurg's treatise is the only independent source for this and for a companion work, H. 337/1 (*W. 116/16*), neither of which seems completely characteristic of Emanuel Bach. Miesner identified them, apparently

without further documentation, as the two pieces listed in *NV* (without thematic identification) as keyboard solos 79/4-5. But the questions which Hays raises in her Commentary, pp. 135-40, regarding their authenticity seem fully justified.

55. Koch reproduces most of the slow movement of Symphony no. 42 in keyboard score, *Versuch* III: 179-90.

56. Ritzel, p. 54. Cf. the "incomplete recapitulation" in the sixth of LaRue's hypothetical sonata forms (*Guidelines*, pp. 188-9).

57. Stevens, "An Eighteenth-Century Description of Concerto First Movement Form," *JAMS* 24 (1971): 89.

58. Joseph Riepel, *Anfangsgründe zur musicalischen Setzkunst* (Frankfurt and Leipzig, 1755), p. 94, discussed by Ritzel, pp. 72-5.

59. *JAMS* 24: 95.

60. *Versuch* III: 332-3.

61. Sulzer, "Sonate," *Allgemeine Theorie* IV: 425, cited by Koch, *Versuch* III: 330.

62. As Leon Crickmore does in his article "C.P.E. Bach's Harpsichord Concertos," *Music and Letters* 39 (1958): 231-2.

63. Koch's effort to resolve the ambiguity in the *Lexikon* is the subject of the article by Shelley Davis (see Note 2-65).

Chapter 4

1. *Sonata in the Classic Era*, p. 29.

2. "C.P.E. Bach His Mark," *College Music Symposium* 19 (1979): 154-61.

3. "The Keyboard Sonatas," p. 194.

4. "C. Ph. E. Bachs Variationwerke," *Revue belge de musicologie* 6 (1952): 210.

5. Bach almost never begins the "recapitulation" with anything other than the opening of the principal theme. In this case the retransition elides into the third section, omitting the usual strong articulation of the return.

6. *The Keyboard Concertos*, p. 61.

7. The possibility that Emanuel had a hand in transcribing one version of the keyboard concerto BWV 1052 is discussed by Wade, *The Keyboard Concertos*, pp. 114-17. Though Wade casts doubt on Emanuel's authorship of the version BWV 1052a, the point remains that Sebastian's students were familiar with his usual method of transcription. The more elaborate methods uniquely adopted in the Triple Concerto, BWV 1044, have hitherto been taken as evidence in favor of Sebastian's authorship of this version, but the varied reprises and the uncharacteristically high notes for the keyboard in the slow movement suggest that here one or more students at least collaborated with him.

8. Preface to the edition by Fritz Oberdorffer (Kassel: Bärenreiter, 1949).

9. "The Keyboard Sonatas," p. 190.

10. *The Classical Style*, p. 48.

11. The fragment, on a page in the autograph score containing the final version (P 354), gives a generally simpler version of mm. 74-7 and 83-108: the return occurs at m. 72. In

reconstructing the opening of the movement in the original version I have assumed a) that the original followed the same form as the revision, and b) that m. 76 of the original constituted a sequential repetition of m. 72, as it does (with altered figuration) in the final version. For a somewhat different interpretation, see Wade, *The Keyboard Concertos,*, p. 99.

12.   Felix Salzer, "Über die Bedeutung der Ornamentik in Philipp Emanuel Bachs Klavierwerken," *Zeitschrift für Musikwissenschaft* 12 (1929-30): 398-418, argues that even the smallest of the *Spielmanieren*—e.g. the upper neighbor and its "resolution" within a single trill—form lines which reflect identical motives found at higher structural levels. In this, argues Salzer, lies the significance of Bach's local ornamentation. The underlying doctrine, the identity of motivic and contrapuntal processes at all structural levels of a work, is a fixture of Schenkerian analysis which unfortunately trivializes the concept of motive. It depends on the simplistic view of a motive as merely "a recurring series of tones" which does not necessarily receive any particular rhythmic shape or articulation, or have any function beyond the composing-out of a line or harmony. See Schenker's *Harmony,* trans. Elisabeth Borgeses (Chicago: University of Chicago Press, 1954), p. 4.

13.   That the trill sign in the string parts indicates the same ornament as the turn in the keyboard part is confirmed by Bach in the *Versuch* I: 56-7. Louis Bagger makes a similar observation in *Notes* 34 (1978): 971, and the same convention can be observed throughout Bach's autographs as well as in other sources from the Bach circle.

14.   "Haydn's Chamber Music," *The Main Stream of Music and Other Essays* (New York: Oxford University Press, 1949), p. 28.

15.   For example, two sonata movements, H. 84 (*W. 70/3*) 1 and H. 136 (*W. 50/1*) 3, both in F, share identical formal schemes in the outer sections, but only the latter introduces new motivic material in the sequential passage following the return.

Chapter 5

1.   "The Keyboard Sonatas," pp. 191-3.

2.   Ibid., p. 90.

3.   *BJ* 12: 70.

4.   "The Keyboard Sonatas," p. 187.

5.   Isolated halves of measures in common time are not unknown in works of other Baroque and pre-Classical composers, at least at cadences; cf. Corelli, Trio-Sonata op. 2, no. 2, third movement, or Leclair, Violin Sonata op. 9, no. 10, second movement.

6.   *The Classical Style*, p. 90. Rosen's observation applies to certain types of movement with a regular pulse,but obviously not to movements based on a strongly characterized dance rhythm like the sarabande.

7.   Berg, "The Keyboard Sonatas," p. 123.

8.   Ibid., p. 176.

9.   *The Classical Style*, p. 58.

10.   Schmid, *Kammermusik*, p, 49.

11.   "The Keyboard Sonatas," pp. 92-3.

12.   See Note 3-60.

13. The term was introduced into English by Oliver Strunk, "Haydn's Divertimenti for Baryton, Viola and Bass," *MQ* 18 (1932): 236.

14. The use of the main theme at the end of the second section of a sonata is fairly common and is a reference to the ritornello which follows the second solo section in a concerto or aria.

15. A similar return, but from D *major* to E, occurs in the final movement of the Sonata H. 281 (*W. 59/1*).

16. The work also occurs in a version for harpsichord and flute, H. 507 (*W. 84*).

17. E.g. Berg, "The Keyboard Sonatas," p. 122.

18. First published in 1730, and likewise employing hand-crossings. Another example of this rather specialized genre is the minuet in Friedemann's Suite in G minor, F. 24 (mod. ed. in *TP*).

19. "The Keyboard Sonatas," p. 122.

20. Marpurg, *Anleitung*, p. 40; Löhlein, *Clavier-Schule* II: 129, 131.

21. Among them the *Duetti* with keyboard of Christoph Schaffrath and the Sonata in E-flat for cembalo and flute attributed to J.S. Bach (BWV 1031). See David Fuller, "Accompanied Keyboard Music," *MQ* 60 (1976): 228. The prototype for such movements is perhaps the first movement of the Sonata in A for harpsichord and flute, BWV 1032, certainly by Sebastian Bach although surviving only in fragmentary form.

22. *Sonata à tre in G♯ con 2. Themata del Sigree.* Carl Em. Graun, for violin or flute, violin, and continuo, in SPK 8295/12. I am grateful to David Sheldon for furnishing a copy of this work.

23. The preface opens the print *Zwey Trio* (Nuremburg, 1751), which includes H. 579 and another far less interesting work for flute, violin, and continuo in B-flat, H. 578 (*W. 161/2*).

24. A. Peter Brown, "Approaching Musical Classicism," *College Music Symposium* 20/1 (Spring, 1980): 22.

25. Ibid., 21.

26. *The Classical Style*, p. 48.

27. Ibid., p. 150.

28. "Sonatenform-Probleme," *Festshrift Friedrich Blume zum 70. Geburtstag*, ed. Anna Amalie Abert and Wilhelm Pfannkuch (Kassel: Bärenreiter, 1963), pp. 226 ff.

29. The original set of six keyboard pieces is not listed as such in *WV*; the title, date, and grouping are indicated in *NV*, where the set constitutes item 175 among the keyboard works. All but the fifth piece exist in later versions for accompanied keyboard, keyboard duet, or wind band; the sixth piece exists as well in an alternate version for solo keyboard. The entire complex of sixteen distinct pieces furnishes many instructive examples of Bach's manner of varying material and expanding simple binary forms.

30. *BJ* 12: 75-8.

31. *Versuch* I: 129,

32. "The Keyboard Sonatas," pp. 126-8.

33. For an example in which Bach fails to start the last movement in the expected key, see Ex. 6-23.

34.   *The Main Stream of Music*, p. 28.

35.   *Guidelines*, pp. 46-7.

Chapter 6

1.   Berg, "The Keyboard Sonatas," pp. 115-6, 148.

2.   Ibid., p. 139.

3.   On this important point, see *The Classical Style*, pp. 26 ff. Although some Classical works (particularly those in minor keys) find alternatives to the tonic/dominant polarity, the dependence of each movement on some polar opposition of keys, articulated by the two principal themes of the exposition, seems basic to most Classical sonata forms.

4.   As Brown does in *College Music Symposium* 20/1: 22. The expression "migrating tonality" is from LaRue, *Guidelines*, p. 52.

5.   *The Classical Style*, p. 383.

6.   Bach's *Versuch* II: 18-19 notes the possibility of using either a single large flat or "two flats" (*zwey Been*) to indicate the double-flat when it occurs in a figured bass signature, although Bach admits that the single large flat is "not yet" in wide use despite its convenience. Elsewhere Bach seems to have taken pains to avoid the misunderstanding found in modern editions, as shown in the two autograph scores of the slow movement of the Concerto H. 441 *(W. 31)*. P 711, which gives the *Auszierungen zum Adagio*, notates the B-double-flat in the bass at m. 31 in the modern manner. At the corresponding point in the original version, P 352, there is a huge single flat the head of which covers dearly the entire width of the staff.

7.   The double-flats appear correctly in the edition in *TP*. There appear to be no independent sources of the sonata apart from the two printings of the first edition (one employing soprano clef for the right hand, the other employing treble). Schenker edited the sonata in the second volume of pieces which he selected from Bach's *Kenner und Liebhaber* series to illustrate his *Beitrag zur Ornamentik* (Vienna: Universal, 1902).

8.   This relationship between sections, very rare in the works of Bach and other northern composers, is common in the sonatas of Domenico Scarlatti, in which the part after the double-bar is sometimes little more than a reprise of the latter portion of the first part,

9.   The chord-tones in the first beat of m. 2 (reading up from the bass) are E, B and D-flat. The melodic figure in the treble is a written-out example of the dotted *Anschlag*, an ornament typical of the *empfindsam* style in its long delay of the chord-tone, which is reduced to an apparent passing note at the very end of the beat. The same interpretation applies in m. 38 as well, but there the chord on the downbeat is itself an appoggiatura to the dominant-seven on F sounded on the second beat.

10.   Bach reveals his fascination with diminished octaves and other exotic intervals at various points in the chapters on continuo realization in the second volume of the *Versuch*. Such cross-relations are relatively common in the *empfindsam* style, particularly in the cadential formula illustrated at the close of the Largo in Ex. 6-23.

11.   Forkel; see Note 3-7.

12.   *Versuch*, p. 156.

13.   The cadenzas required in the six concertos of W. 43 are all written out in the keyboard part. Additional cadenzas for earlier concertos are collected in the *80 Clavier-Cadenzen* H. 264 (*W.

120), preserved in *B* Bc U5871. A few cadenzas for the solo sonatas occur among the *Veränderungen und Auszierungen* of H. 166 (*W. 68*). These cadenzas usually consist of an expressive prolongation of the I6/4-chord, usually without any reference to the thematic material of the movement; hence a considerable number of the cadenzas in H. 264 are identified only by key and tempo, and evidently were not intended for a specific concerto.

14.   St 578, according to Kast. The cancellation of the repeat signs in the autograph flute parts of St 238 was reported by Richard M. Jacobs, "The Chamber Ensembles of C.P.E. Bach using Two or More Wind Instruments," diss., Iowa State University, 1964, p. 84 fn. This casts in doubt the conclusion of Ernst Suchalla, in *Die Orchestersinfonien Carl Philipp Emanuel Bachs* (Augsburg: Blasaditsch, 1968), p. 22, that the repeat-sign in the keyboard reduction was a copyist's arbitrary decision. The only other opening movements in symphonic style by Bach which include repetitions, outside of solo keyboard sonatas, are in the two *sinfonie* for trio ensembles H. 507 (*W. 74*) and H. 582 (*W. 156*). Repetitions also occur in the little symphony, H. 667 (*Wq, n.v. 69*) which Suchalla (pp. 127 ff) identifies as the one which Bach and his student von Lobkowitz composed jointly by writing alternate measures. All three works date from the early 1750's, before Bach's serious efforts in the genre. On Lobkowitz, see Wade's note in her annotated facsimile edition of *NV*, p. 148.

15.   *Essays in Musical Analysis* VI: 8-9.

16.   Hardly a peculiarity of Bach's style, similar movements are common in the operatic *sinfonie* of the eighteenth century, a point Tovey must have had in mind in his reference (see prev ious note) to Graun's overtures. Other examples are found in the works of Haydn (Overture to *Lo speziale*) and Mozart (Symphony, K. 318).

17.   This concerto exists in versions for flute, as H. 438 (*W. 168*), and for cello, as H. 439 (*W. 172*). The three versions, which differ mainly in the solo part, are presented simultaneously in the edition by Hans Maria Kneihs (London: Eulenburg, 1967).

18.   See Note 3-60.

19.   Bach's sonatas for gamba and continuo date from 1745 and 1746, respectively, and must have been written for one of those late masters of the instrument (among them C.F. Abel) whose careers reached up to and beyond the middle of the eighteenth century. Bach, like Abel, apparently wrote the solo part of his gamba sonatas in treble clef; this may account for the error in *NV* which assigns H. 558 to the flute. (The same convention applied in several sources of Sebastian Bach's D-major gamba sonata, BWV 1028, is probably the source of references to a violin version of the work. In both cases the notation of a few very low passages in bass clef makes performance on the alternative instrment unlikely.) There are a few virtuosic works by J.G. Graun for gamba and obligato keyboard; these, like Emanuel's relatively mild sonata for the same combination, H. 510 (*W, 88*) of 1759, exist in alternate versions for viola. Might some of these works have been written for Abel? The latter had close family ties with Bach; but Abel was in Dresden until 1757 or 1758, and political conditions then were not auspicious for a member of the Saxon court to be visiting Berlin.

20.   *The Classical Style*, p. 115.

21.   Suchalla, p. 49.

22.   This sonata movement is a keyboard reduction of the slow movement of the E-minor symphony, H. 652 (*W. 177*), written a year earlier in 1756. There is a lost keyboard version of the entire symphony, H. 115 (*W. 122/3*). It seems reasonable to trace the sonata movement to the keyboard version of the symphony; or is the latter simply the result of a cataloguer's confusion with the former?

23. "jetzt so herrschenden und beliebten Musikgattung." *Musikalisch-Kritische Bibliothek* (Gotha, 1778-9: rpt., Hildesheim: Olm, 1964) II: 281.

24. See note 2-23.

25. See note 3-7.

26. Bach's tempo markings for the two last movements raise the question of which is faster: *Andante* or *Andantino grazioso*? Despite disagreement among eighteenth-century writers, Koch's definition in the *Lexikon* of *Andantino* as "etwas geschwinder...als Andante" seems to apply here.

27. Actually the *Anschlag* can be traced back to the double appoggiaturas in the retransition of the Andante (Ex. 5-33).

28. In these works, however, material from one or more sections recurs at several different points in the course of the piece.

29. Kurt von Fischer, *Revue belge* 6: 217, speaks of the variation sets H. 535 (*W. 79*) and H. 534 (*W. 91/4*) as tending "toward a conception of the whole" (*zu einer Ganzheit*). H. 534 dates from 1777, H. 535 from 1781.

30. Possibly it was popular demand for shorter slow movements that first led to their being relegated to the role of simple bridge passages, at least in Bach's published sonatas. A letter to Breitkopf (apparently from 1785; quoted by Hase, *BJ* 8: 101) mentions the brevity of the slow movement as a selling point of the sonata H. 209 (*W. 60*), which Breitkopf published later that year. Similar very brief slow movements occur in the first two of the *Sonates à l'usage des dames*, H. 204 and 205 (*W. 54/1-2*).

31. *Essays in Musical Analysis* VI: 11. Tovey compares the design of the symphony unfavorably with that of Haydn's sonata Hob. XVI: 51, which likewise has a slow movement in the Neapolitan but without transition passages.

32. The fanciful hermeneutic interpretation of the sonata given by Cramer (see Note 3-6) makes no reference to the work's odd key structure.

33. One other sonata, H. 165 (*W. 53/5*), ends in a key different from the one in which it begins; the first movement in C is followed by two movements in A minor, a relatively close tonality. One might also count in this category the six one-movement *neue Sonatinen*, H. 292-7 (*W. 63/7-12*), which are listed as two sets of three pieces each in *NV* (as Berg notes, "The Keyboard Sonatas," p. 293).

Chapter 7

1. In his review of the piano trios of W. 90. *Musikalisch-Kritsche Bibliothek* II: 278.

2. Because these pieces are readily available in several editions (including Schenker's, for the Rondo), the scores are not reproduced here, although the reader is urged to have copies on hand for consultation while reading this chapter.

3. August Frederic Christopher Kollmann, *An Essay on Practical Musical Composition* (London, 1799; rpt. New York: Da Capo, 1973), illustrates the "improper rondo" with the final movement of Bach's piano trio H. 524 (*W. 90/2*). This movement is one of several in the piano trios which resemble the late rondos for solo keyboard. See also William S. Cole, "Rondos, Proper and Improper," *Music and Letters* 51 (1970): 388-99.

4. "Bach and Handel," *Keyboard Music*, ed. Matthews, p. 106. Cole, *Music and Letters* 51: 389, makes a similar comparison with the fantasia.

5. The variation technique here resembles the procedure by which Bach expanded the outer sections of the sonata H. 16 (*W. 65/7*) 1.

6. Here, as well as in the last two measures of the retransition phrase, the chromaticism and the written-out dissolution of the meter recall the long adagio measure at bar 31.

7. This breaking of the surface rhythm prior to the return is characteristic of Bach's sonata forms (cf. Ex. 5-8). The closest Bach comes in a rondo to a dramatic return is in the work in B-flat, H. 267 (*W. 58/5*), but even there the retransition comes to rest briefly in a half-cadence after fourteen measures of climactic figuration over a dominant pedal.

8. The C major reached at the end of the second part of the B section is not, of course, heard as a return to the tonic of the work but in relation to the E-minor of the B section.

9. Formal considerations of this sort have little place in Schenker-influenced modes of analysis, although they would seem to lie at the basis of the Schenkerian doctrine of interruption (used to explain repetitions, among other things). But formal principles, that is, what Leonard Meyer calls "conformant relationships," are essential in establishing the coherence of works that purely reductive analysis finds incoherent, that is, not reducible to a germinal *Ursatz*. Meyer discusses conformant relationships in "Toward a Theory of Style," *The Concept of Style*, ed. Berel Lang (N.p.: University of Pennsylvania Press, 1979), pp. 14-18.

10. Cf, the first movement of the *Programm-Trio*, in which the two "characters" consistently interrupt each other (Ex. 5-25).

11. The B-flat minor heard at the beginning of the first prestissimo passage (bar 19) is the product of an enharmonic reinterpretation of the diminished chord in the preceding measure. The passage at bar 31 resolves that diminished chord to G minor, the key originally prepared.

12. In the rondo this is accomplished far less smoothly, by the short and rather dull retransition phrase.

13. Cf. Note 1-10.

Chapter 8

1. Indicated by the *unisono* close of the ritornello in the third movement and similar theatrical gestures.

2. In the final paragraph of the first volume. In his translation, p. 166, Mitchell adds a footnote quoting Bach's thoughts on the same matter in the foreword to the *Reprisen-Sonaten* (W. 50).

3. Given in the ms collection of varied reprises, H. 164 (*W. 68*).

Bibliography

Anonymous. Reviews of C.P.E. Bach, Variations H. 14 (*W. 118/7*) and H. 263 (*W. 118/9*). *Allgemeine musikalische Zeitung* 6/15 (January 11, 1804): 243-4.

Apel, Willi. *French Secular Music of the Late Fourteenth Century.* Cambridge, Mass.: Mediaeval Academy of America, 1950.

_____. *The Notation of Polyphonic Music.* 5th ed. Cambridge, Mass.: The Mediaeval Academy of America, 1961.

Bach, Carl Philipp Emanuel. *Versuch über die wahre Art das Clavier zu spielen.* 2 vols. Berlin, 1753-62. Facs. rpt. ed. Lothar Hoffmann-Erbrecht. Leipzig: Breitkopf und Härtel, 1976. Trans. as *Essay on the True Art of Playing Keyboard Instruments* by William J. Mitchell, New York: Norton, 1949.

_____. *Verzeichniss des musikalischen Nachlasses des verstorbenen Capellmeisters Carl Philipp Emanuel Bach.* Hamburg, 1790. Ed. Heinrich Miesner, *BJ* 35 (1938): 103-36, 36 (1939): 81-112, 37 (1940-48): 161-81. Facs. rpt. annotated, with a preface, by Rachel W. Wade, as *The Catalog of Carl Philipp Emanuel Bach's Estate.* New York: Garland, 1981.

_____ [Autobiography] in the German ed. of Burney's *Present State of Music* (q.v,), facs. rpt. ed. William S. Newman, as *Carl Philipp Emanuel Bach's Autobiography.* Hilversum: Knuf, 1967.

Bagger, Louis. Review of C.P.E. Bach, Concerto H. 441 (*W. 31*), ed. Gyorgy Balla in *Nagels Musik-Archiv* 253 (Kassel: Bärenreiter, 1976). *Notes* 34 (1978): 970-2.

Barford, Philip Trevelyan. *The Keyboard Music of C.P.E. Bach Considered in Relation to his Musical Aesthetic and the Rise of the Sonata Principle.* New York: October House, 1965. Reviewed by David Fuller in *Notes* 23 (1967): 726-7, and by Stanley Sadie in *Musical Times* 107 (1966): 35-7.

_____. "The Sonata-Principle: A Study of Musical Thought in the Eighteenth century." *Music Review* 13 (1952): 255-63.

Benecke, Rolf. "Johann Christoph Friedrich Bach." *MGG* I (1949-51): 956-60.

Berg, Darrell Matthews. "The Keyboard Sonatas of C.P.E. Bach: An Expression of the Mannerist Principle." Diss., State University of New York at Buffalo, 1975.

_____. "Toward a Catalog of the Keyboard Sonatas of C.P.E. Bach," *JAMS* 32 (1979): 276-303.

Beurmann, Erich Herbert. Die Klaviersonaten Carl Philipp Emanuel Bachs. Diss., Georg-August Universität, Göttingen, 1952.

_____. "Die Reprisensonaten Carl Philipp Emanuel Bachs." *Archiv für Musikwissenschaft* 13 (1956): 168-79.

Bitter, C.H. *Carl Philipp Emanuel Bach und Wilhelm Friedemann Bach und deren Brüder.* 2 vols. Berlin: W. Müller, 1868. Facs. rpt., Leipzig: Zentralantiquariat, 1973.

Brown, A. Peter. "Approaching Musical Classicism," *College Music Symposium* 20/1 (Spr., 1980): 7-48.

Buck, Charles H. "Revisions in Early Classical Concertos of C. P.E. Bach: Revisions from a New Source," *JAMS* 29 (1976): 127-32. Cf. reply by Rachel W. Wade in *JAMS* 30 (1977): 162-4.

Bukofzer, Manfred. "Allegory in Baroque Music." *Journal of the Warburg and Courtauld Institutes* 3 (1939-40): 1-22.

X Burney, Charles. *The Present State of Music in Germany, the Netherlands and the United Provinces.* 2 vols. London, 1775. Facs. rpt., New York: Broude, 1969. Trans. into German as *Carl Burney's der Musik Doctors Tagebuch einer musikalische Reisen* by C.D. Ebeling and J.J.C. Bode. 3 vols. Hamburg, 1773. Facs. rpt. ed. Richard Schalle. Kassel: Bärenreiter, 1959.

Campbell, Robert Gordon. *Johnn Gottfried Müthel, 1728-1788.* Diss., Indiana University, 1966.

Canave, Pas Corazon G. *A Re-Evaluation of the Role Played by Carl Philipp Emmanuel [sic] Bach in the Development of the Clavier Sonata.* Washington: Catholic University of America Press, 1956. Reviewed by William S. Newman. *Notes* 14 (1956): 363-4.

Clark, Stephen L. "The Occasional Choral Works of C.P.E. Bach." Diss., Princeton University (in progress).

Clercx, Suzanne. "La forme du rondo chez Carl Philipp Emanuel Bach." *Revue de musicologie* 16 (1935): 148-67.

Cohen, Peter. *Theorie und Praxis der Clavierästhetik Carl Philipp Bachs.* Hamburg: Wagner, 1974.

Cole, William S. "Rondos, Proper and Improper." *Music and Letters* 51 (1970): 388-99.

Cramer, Carl Friedrich. *Magazin der Musik.* Hamburg, 1783-4. Facs. rpt., Hildesheim: Olms, 1971.

Crickmore, Leon. "C.P.E. Bach's Harpsichord Concertos." *Music and Letters* 39 (1958): 227-41.

Cudworth, Charles L. "Ye Olde Spuriosity Shoppe, or Put It In the Anhang." *Notes* 12 (1955): 25-40, 533-55.

Dahlhaus, Carl. *Fundamentals of Music History.* Trans. J.B. Robingon. London: Cambridge University Press, 1983.

Darbellay, Étienne. Preface to *C.P.E. Bach: Sechs Sonaten mit veränderten Reprisen [W. 50].* Winterthur: Amadeus, 1976.

David, Hans, and Arthur Mendel, eds. *The Bach Reader.* Rev. ed. New York: Norton, 1966.

Davis, Shelley, "J.G. Lang and the Early Classical Keyboard Concerto." *MQ* 56 (1980): 21-52.

_____. "H.C. Koch, the Classic Concerto, and the Sonata-Form Retransition." *Journal of Musicology* 2 (1983): 45-61.

Deutsch, Otto. *Mozart: A Documentary Biography.* 2d ed. Stanford: Stanford University Press, 1966.

Eppstein, Hans. *Studien über J.S. Bachs Sonaten für ein Melodie-Instrument und obligato Cembalo.* Uppsala: Almquist und Wiksell, 1966.

Falck, Martin. *Wilhelm Friedemann Bach: Sein Leben und seine Werke.* Leipzig: Kahnt, 1913.

Fischer, Kurt. "Arietta variata." *Studies in Eighteenth-Century Music: A Tribute to Karl Geiringer on his Seventieth Birthday.* Ed. H.C. Robbins Landon in collaboration with Roger E. Chapman. London: Allen and Unwin, 1970. Pp. 224-35.

_____. "C.Ph. E. Bachs Variationwerke." *Revue belge de musicologie* 6 (1952): 190-218.

Forkel, Johann Nicolaus. *Musikalisch-Kritische Bibliothek.* 3 vols. Gotha, 1778-9. Facs. rpt., Hildesheim: Olms, 1964.

_____. *Musikalischer Almanach für Deutschland auf das Jahr 1783.* Leipzig, 1784. Facs. rpt., Hildesheim: Olms, 1974.

_____. *Musikalischer Almanach für Deutschland auf das Jahr 1784.* Leipzig, 1789. Facs. rpt., Hildesheim: Olms, 1974.

Franck, Wolf. "Musicology and Its Founder, Johann Nicolaus Forkel (1749-1818)." *MQ* 35 (1949): 588-609.

Fuller, David. "Accompanied Keyboard Music." *MQ* 60 (1974): 222-45.

_____. Review of Barford (q.v.).

Godt, Irving. "C.P.E. Bach His Mark." *College Music Symposium* 19/2 (Fall, 1979): 154-61.

Haag, Charles R. "The Keyboard Concertos of Carl Philipp Emanuel Bach." Diss., University of California at Los Angeles, 1956.

Hager, Nancy Barnes. "Rhythm and Voice-Leading as a Facet of Style: Keyboard Works of J.S. Bach, C.P.E. Bach, and Mozart." Diss., City University of New York, 1978.

Hase, Hermann von. "Carl Philipp Emanuel Bach und Joh. Gottl. Im. Breitkopf." *BJ* 8 (1911): 86-104.

Hays, Elizabeth Loretta. "F.W. Marpurg's *Anleitung zum Clavierspielen* (Berlin, 1755) and *Principes du clavecin* (Berlin, 1756): Translation and Commentary." Diss,, Stanford University, 1976.

Heimes, Klaus Ferdinand. "The Ternary Sonata Principle before 1742." *Acta musicologica* 45 (1973): 222-48.

Heinichen, Johann David. *Der Generalbass in der Composition*. Dresden, 1728.

Helm, E. Eugene. Articles on C.P.E., J.C.F., and W.F. Bach, and on the Graun family, in *New Grove*.

————. *Music at the Court of Frederick the Great*. Norman: University of Oklahoma Press, 1960.

————. "Six Random Measures of C.P.E. Bach." *JMT* 10 (1966): 139-50.

————, *Thematic Catalog of the Works of Carl Philipp Emanuel Bach*. New Haven: Yale University Press (in press).

Hoffmann-Erbrecht, Lothar. "Sturm und Drang in der deutschen Klaviermusik von 1750-1763." *Musikforschung* 10 (1957): 466-79.

Jacobi, Erwin R. "Das Autograph C.Ph.E. Bachs Doppelkonzert in Es-dur für Cembalo, Fortepiano und Orchester (Wq. 47, Hamburg 1786)." *Musikforschung* 12 (1959): 488-9.

————. "Five Hitherto Unknown Letters from C.P.E. Bach to J.J.H. Westphal." *JAMS* 23 (1970): 119-27.

————. "Three Additional Letters from C.P.E. Bach to J.J.H. Westphal." *JAMS* 27 (1974): 119-25.

Jacobs, Richard M. "The Chamber Ensembles of C.P.E. Bach using Two or More Wind Instruments." Diss., Iowa State University, 1964.

Jonas, Oswald. Preface to *C.P.E. Bach: Short and Easy Piano Pieces with Varied Reprises [W. 113-14]*. Vienna: Universal, 1962.

Jurisch, Herta. "Zur Dynamik im Klavierwerk Ph.E. Bachs." *Bericht über den Internationalen Musikwissenschaftlichen Kongress Kassel 1962*. Ed. Georg Reichert and Martin Just. Kassel: Bärenreiter, 1963. Pp. 178-81.

Kalib, Sylvan. "Thirteen Essays from the Three Yearbooks 'Das Meisterwerk in der Musik' by Heinrich Schenker: An Annotated Translation." Diss., University of Michigan, 1977.

Kast, Paul. *Die Bach-Handschriften der Berliner Staatsbibliothek*. Trossingen: Hohner, 1958.

Kirnberger, Johann Philipp. *Die Kunst des reinen Satzes*. 2 vols. Berlin and Königsberg, 1771-9. Facs. rpt., Hildesheim: Olms, 1968. Trans. of vol. 1 and vol. 2, part 1, as *The Art of Strict Musical Composition*, by Jurgen Thym and David Beach. New Haven: Yale University Press, 1982.

————. *Gedanken über die verschiedenen Lehrarten in der Komposition als Vorbereitung zur Fugenkenntniss*. Vienna, 1782.

————. *Sonaten aus'm Ermel zu schüddeln*. Berlin, 1783. Facs. rpt. and trans. as "Kirnberger's 'Method for Tossing Off Sonatas'," *MQ* 47 (1961): 517-25.

Kobayashi, Toshitake. "Neuerkenntnisse zu einigen Bach-Quellen an handschriftkündlicher Untersuchungen." *BJ* 64 (1978): 43-60.

Koch, Heinrich Christoph. *Musikalisches Lexikon*. Frankfurt, 1802. Facs. rpt., Hildesheim: Olms, 1964.

————. *Versuch einer Anleitung zur Composition.* 3 vols. Rudolstadt, 1782, and Berlin, 1787-93. Facs. rpt., Hildesheim: Olms, 1969.

Kollmann, August Frederic Christopher. *An Essay on Practical Musical Composition.* London, 1799. Facs. rpt. with introd. by Imogene Horsley, New York: Da Capo, 1973.

Landon, H.C. Robbins. *Haydn: Chronicle and Works.* 5 vols. Bloomington: Indiana University Press, 1978-80.

LaRue, Jan. *Guidelines for Style Analysis.* New York: Norton, 1970.

————. "Symphonie. Norddeutschland." *MGG* XII: 1828-31.

Lee, Douglas Allen. "The Instrumental Works of Christoph Nichelmann." Diss., University of Michigan, 1968.

————. "Some Embellished Versions of Sonatas by Franz Benda." *MQ* 62 (1976): 58-71.

Löhlein, Georg Simon. *Clavier-Schule oder kurze und gründliche Anweisung zur Melodie und Harmonie.* Leipzig, 1765.

Longyear, Rey M. "Binary Variants of Early Classical Sonata Form." *JMT* 13 (1969): 162-85.

Louwenaar, Karyl June. "The Keyboard Concertos of Christoph Schaffrath (1709-1763)." D.M.A. diss., Eastman School of Music of the University of Rochester, 1974.

Maniates, Maria Rika. *Mannerism in Italian Music and Culture, 1530-1630.* Chapel Hill: University of North Carolina Press, 1979.

Marpurg, Friedrich Wilhelm. *Abhandlung von der Fuge.* 2 vols. Berlin, 1753. Facs. rpt,, Hildesheim: Olms, 1970.

————. *Anleitung zum Clavierspielen. Zweyte verbesserte Auflage.* Berlin, 1765. Facs. rpt., New York: Broude, 1969. Trans. Elizabeth Loretta Hays (q.v.).

————. *Der critische Musicus an der Spee . . . erster Band.* Berlin, 1749. Facs. rpt., Hildesheim: Olms, 1970.

————. *Handbuch bey dem Generalbasse in der Komposition.* 2 vols. Berlin, 1757-69.

————. *Kritische Briefe über die Tonkunst.* 3 vols. Berlin, 1759-64. Facs. rpt., Hildesheim: Olms, 1974.

————. *Principes du clavecin.* Berlin, 1756. Facs. rpt., Geneva: Minkoff, 1974. Trans. Elizabeth Loretta Hays (q.v.).

Marshall, Robert. "Bach the Progressive." *MQ* 62 (1976): 313-57.

————. *The Compositional Process of J.S. Bach: A Study of the Autograph Scores of the Vocal Works.* 2 vols. Princeton: Princeton University Press, 1972.

Mattheson, Johann. *Grosse General-Bass-Schule.* Hamburg, 1731. Facs. rpt., Hildesheim: Olms, 1968.

————. *Der vollkommene Capellmeister.* Hamburg, 1739. Facs. rpt. ed. Margarethe Riemann. Kassel: Bärenreiter, 1954. Trans. as *Johann Mattheson's* Der vollkommene Capellmeister: *A Revised Translation with Critical Commentary* by Ernest C. Harris. Ann Arbor: UMI Research Press, 1981.

Mersmann, Hans. "Ein Programmtrio Karl Philipp Emanuel Bachs." *BJ* 14 (1917): 137-72.

Meyer, Leonard. "Toward a Theory of Style." *The Concept of Style,* ed. Berel Lang. N.p.: University of Pennsylvania Press, 1979. Pp. 14-18.

Miesner, Heinrich. "Aus der Umwelt Philipp Emanuel Bachs." *BJ* 34 (1937): 132-43.

————. *Philipp Emanuel Bach in Hamburg: Beiträge zu seiner Biographie und zur Musikgeschichte seiner Zeit.* Wiesbaden: Breitkopf und Härtel, 1929.

————. "Philipp Emanuel Bach's musikalischer Nachlass." *BJ* 35 (1938): 103-36, 36 (1939): 81-112, and 37 (1940-48): 161-81.

Mitchell, William J. "Chord and Context in Eighteenth-Century Theory." *JMT* 16 (1963): 221-39.

Newman, William S., ed. *Carl Philipp Emanuel Bach's Autobiography—1773.* Hilversum: Knuf. 1967.

————. "Emanuel Bach's Autobiography." *MQ* 51 (1965): 363-72.

✓ _____. "The Keyboard Sonatas of Bach's Sons and Their Relation to the Classic Sonata Concept." *Proceedings for 1949, Music Teachers National Association*: 236-48.

_____. "Kirnberger's 'Method for Tossing Off Sonatas'." *MQ* 47 (1961): 517-25.

_____. "The Recognition of Sonata Form by Theorists of the Eighteenth and Nineteenth Centuries." *Papers of the AMS* (1941: published 1946): 21-9.

_____. Review of Canave (q.v.).

_____. *The Sonata in the Classic Era*. 2d ed. New York: Norton, 1972.

Plamenac, Dragan. "New Light on the Last Years of Carl Philipp Emanuel Bach." *MQ* 35 (1949): 565-87.

Quantz, Johann Joachim. *Versuch einer Anweisung die Flöte traversiere zu spielen*. Berlin, 1752. Facs. rpt. of the 3d ed. (Berlin, 1789), Kassel: Bärenreiter, 1953. Trans. as *An Essay on Playing the Flute* by Edward J. Reilly, London: Faber, 1966.

Ratner, Leonard. *Classic Music: Expression, Form, and Style*. New York: Schirmer Books, 1980.

_____. "Eighteenth-Century Theories of Musical Period Structure." *MQ* 42 (1956): 439-54.

_____. "Harmonic Aspects of Classical Form." *JAMS* 2 (1949): 159-68.

Ritzel, Fred. *Die Entwicklung der "Sonatenform" im musiktheroretischen Schrifftum des 18. und 19. Jahrhunderts*. 2d ed. Wiesbaden: Breitkopf und Härtel, 1969.

Rose, Gloria. "Father and Son: Some Attributions to J.S. Bach by C.P.E. Bach," in *Studies in Eighteenth-Century Music: A Tribute to Karl Geiringer on his Seventieth Birthday*. Ed. H. C. Robbins Landon in collaboration with Roger E. Chapman. London: Allen and Unwin, 1970. Pp. 364-9.

Rose, Juanelva. "The Harmonic Idiom of the Keyboard Works of Carl Philipp Emanuel Bach." Diss., University of California at Santa Barbara, 1970.

Rosen, Charles. "Bach and Handel." *Keyboard Music*, ed. Denis Matthews. New York: Praeger, 1972. Pp. 68-107.

_____. *The Classical Style*. New York: Norton, 1972.

_____. *Sonata Forms*. New York: Norton, 1980.

Sadie, Stanley. Review of Canave (q.v.).

Salzer, Felix. "Über die Bedeutung der Ornamentik in Philipp Emanuel Bachs Klavierwerken." *Zeitschrift für Musikwissenschaft* 12 (1929-30): 398-418.

Scheibe, Johann Adolph. *Der critische Musicus*. 2 vols. Leipzig, 1738-40.

_____. *Der critische Musicus. Neue, vermehrte und verbesserte Auflage*. Leipzig, 1745.

Schenker, Heinrich. *Ein Beitrag zur Ornamentik als Einführung zu C.Ph.E. Bachs Klavierwerke*. Rev. ed. Vienna: Universal, 1908. Trans., as "A Contribution to the Study of Ornamentation," by Hedi Siegal ("based on a preliminary draft by Carl Parrish"), in *The Music Form* 4 (1967): 1-139.

_____. "Die Kunst der Improvisation." *Das Meisterwerk in der Musik*, 3 vols. Munich: Drei Masken, 1925-30. I: 11-40. Trans. Sylvan Kalib (q.v.).

_____. *Neue musikalische Theorien und Phantasien*. Vol. 1. *Harmonielehre*. Vienna: Universal, 1906. Ed. and annotated by Oswald Jonas, and trans., as *Harmony*, by Elisabeth Mann Borghese. Chicago: University of Chicago Press, 1954.

_____. "Ph. Em. Bach: Kurze und leichte Klavierstücke mit veränderten Reprisen, (1766), Nr. 1, *Allegro* [H. 193 (*W. 113/1*)]" and "Ph. Em. Bach: Sonate C-dur (1779) [H. 244 (*W. 55/1*)]. Erster Satz," *Der Tonwille* 4 (1923): 10-14.

Schering, Arnold. "Carl Philipp Emanuel Bach und das 'redende Prinzip' in der Musik." *Jahrbuch der Musikbibliothek Peters für 1937* (1938): 13-29.

Schleuning, Peter. *Die freie Fantasie: Ein Beitrag zur Erforschung der klassischen Klaviermusik*. Göppingen: Kummerle, 1973.

Schmid, Ernst Fritz. *Carl Philipp Emanuel Bach und seine Kammermusik*. Kassel: Bärenreiter, 1931.

———. "Joseph Haydn und Carl Philipp Emanuel Bach." *Zeitschrift für Musikwissenschaft* 14 (1931-2): 299-312.

Schneider, Max. Preface to *Georg Philipp Telemann: Der Tag des Berichts / Ino*, (*Denkmäler deutscher Tonkunst* 28). Leipzig: Breitkopf und Härtel, 1907.

Schulenberg, David. "Composition as Variation: Inquiries into the Compositional Procedures of the Bach Circle of Composers." *Current Musicology* 33 (1984).

Sheldon, David A. "The Galant Style Revisited and Re-evaluated." *Acta* 47 (1975): 240-70.

———. "The Transition from Trio to Cembalo-Obligato Sonata in the Works of J.G. and C.H. Graun." *JAMS* 24 (1971): 395-413.

Steglich, Rudolph. "Carl Philipp Emanuel Bach und der dresdner Kreutzkantor Gottfr. Aug. Homilius im Musikleben ihrer Zeit." *BJ* 12 (1915): 39-145.

Stevens, Jane. "An Eighteenth-Century Description of Concerto First-Movement Form." *JAMS* 24 (1971): 85-95.

———. "The Keyboard Concertos of Carl Philipp Emanuel Bach." Diss., Yale University, 1965.

Suchalla, Ernst. *Die Orchestersinfonien Carl Philipp Emanuel Bachs.* Augsburg: Blasaditsch, 1968.

Sulzer, Johann Georg, ed. *Allgemeine Theorie der schonen Kunst. Neue vermehrte Auflage.* Leipzig, 1792-4. Facs. rpt., Hildesheim: Olms, 1970.

Terry, Miriam. "C.P.E. Bach and J.J.H. Westphal—A Clarification." *JAMS* 22 (1969): 106-15.

Tovey, Sir Donald Francis. *Essays in Musical Analysis.* 6 vols. London: Oxford University Press, 1935.

———. *The Main Stream of Music and Other Essays.* London: Oxford University Press, 1949.

Uldall, Hans. *Das Klavierkonzerte der berliner Schule und ihres Führers Philipp Emanuel Bach.* Leipzig: Breitkopf und Härtel, 1927.

Vrieslander, Otto. *Carl Philipp Emanuel Bach.* Munich: Piper, 1923.

Wade, Rachel W. "Communication," *JAMS* 30 (1977): 162-4.

———. *The Keyboard Concertos of Carl Philipp Emanuel Bach.* Ann Arbor: UMI Research Press, 1981.

Wohlfarth, Hannsdieter. *Johann Christoph Friedrich Bach: Ein Komponist im Vorfeld der Klassik.* Munich: Franck, 1971.

Wotquenne, Alfred. *Thematische Verzeichnis der Werke von Carl Philipp Emanuel Bach, (1714-1788).* Leipzig: Breitkopf und Härtel, 1905.

Wyler, Robert. *Form- und Stiluntersuchungen zur ersten Satz der Klaviersonaten Carl Philipp Emanuel Bachs.* Biel: Graphische Anstalt Schüler, 1960.

Index

References to discussions including musical examples are printed in italics.

DATE